Survival Kit for Multicultural Living

Survival Kit for Multicultural Living

Ellen Summerfield

INTERCULTURAL PRESS, INC.

For information contact
Intercultural Press, Inc.
P.O. Box 700
Yarmouth, Maine 04096 USA
207-846-5168

Book design and production by Patty J. Topel
Cover illustration and design by Tom Brown

Printed in the United States of America

01   00   99   98   2   3   4   5

Library of Congress Cataloging-in-Publication Data

Summerfield, Ellen 1949-
    Survival kit for multicultural living: / Ellen Summerfield.
        p. cm.
    Includes bibliographical references.
    ISBN 1-877864-49-8 (pbk.)
    1. Pluralism (Social sciences)—United States—Handbooks, manuals, etc. 2. Multiculturalism—United States—Handbooks, manuals, etc. I. Title.
E184.A1S96   1997
303.48'2—dc21   97-2357
                                        CIP

To Phil

Permissions

Grateful acknowledgment is made to the following for permission to reprint copyrighted material.

Kirk Anderson, St. Paul, MN, page 54.

Bob Englehart, *The Hartford Courant*, page 61.

Levin Represents, Santa Monica, CA, page 76.

Mike Luckovich and Creators Syndicate, Los Angeles, CA, page 85.

Jeff Shesol, Washington, DC, page 103.

Universal Press Syndicate, Kansas City, MO, page 142.

Table of Contents

Acknowledgments

I express sincere appreciation to Linfield College for helping me to arrange a yearly schedule that allows time for research and writing. This schedule has been successful due in large part to the flexibility and generous assistance of Sandy Soohoo-Refaei and Annette Schoof in the International Programs Office. I also appreciate the fine work of Cynthia Fischer, my research assistant.

For their continuing support and thoughtful critiques, I thank my parents, Helene and Powell Summerfield, and my friend and colleague, Kareen Sturgeon. Phillip Pirages, my husband, has reviewed the manuscript several times and made countless invaluable suggestions on wording and ideas. I will not forget his enthusiasm for the project as a whole and his patience with the most minute details.

Finally, I extend deepest appreciation to the staff at the Intercultural Press: to David Hoopes, for helpful insights and advice in the early stage; to Toby Frank, who has been a source of support and encouragement throughout; to Patty Topel for her design work; and to Judy Carl-Hendrick, whose suggestions for revision were inspired and whose editing has been sensitive and skillful at every point.

Introduction

From time to time, sensational public events like the Rodney King beating and the O. J. Simpson trial remind us of the deep and persisting divisions in our country among different racial and ethnic groups. The connection between these dramatic examples and our own lives may at first seem remote, but in fact each one of us comes into contact every day with people whose backgrounds and values are very different from our own. Whether we welcome this contact or reject it, we no longer have the option to lead lives apart. We are confronted with the challenges and demands of a diverse society at every turn—in our schools and workplaces, in stores and restaurants, in our own neighborhoods and families.

Accepting these challenges and meeting these demands is an important part of the reason for reading this book. If you see the need to *do* something in your own life to improve relations with people unlike yourself, the *Survival Kit* is for you. Here you will find clear, step-by-step guidance in gaining the skills and confidence you need to deal more effectively with a wide variety of people. These people may be of a different race, ethnicity, or nationality from your own. Or perhaps barriers exist between you and others because of religion, gender, class, sexual orientation, disability, or age. All of these human differences—any of which can result in reactions ranging from mild discomfort to hatred and violence—constitute the subject of this book.

What will the *Survival Kit* enable you to do?

- *It will give you a better understanding of the critical multicultural issues of our time.* Why are issues such as affirmative action, immigration, and bilingual education so volatile? What are the arguments on both sides? With a basic grounding in the key issues, you can analyze your feelings and gain a better sense of your own views and position. Note that the emphasis in the *Survival Kit* is not on providing the most up-to-date developments, but on giving you the necessary background to allow you to follow the issues yourself as they continue to evolve. Nor can all the important multicultural issues be covered. But, again, with the fundamental understanding gained here, you should be able to relate more easily to a host of other topics, including controversies over the "bell curve" and Ebonics, debates over race-based election districting and same-sex marriages, and challenges posed to current thinking by multiracial and multiethnic individuals.

  While the *Survival Kit* is written about the United States for Americans of the most diverse backgrounds, international students and scholars and other residents from abroad in the United States may also find it useful as a guide to the complexities of their temporary home.

- *It will help you become more comfortable dealing with, and talking about, sensitive subjects.* Many of us are not used to discussing controversial issues relating to race, ethnicity, gender, and sexuality. But we can't learn much if we don't start to talk. If some of the ideas presented here seem strange, offensive, or disturbing, remember that it's impossible to make significant progress by staying safe and comfortable. If certain issues trouble or concern you, you might wish to discuss them at first with people you know and trust—to practice, in a sense—before expressing your views in public.

- *It will allow you to enter the debates.* Once you have a better grasp of the issues, you can begin to take a stand. Multicultural issues tend to evoke deeply held beliefs and emotions, so you will probably find that it's impossible to stay neutral. While I have my own strong opinions on the issues presented, I admit that I'm always grappling with the other side, and I find I can change my mind on certain points. Thus, I'm not trying to win you to any particular position, but rather to lay out the issues in such a way that you can see what the controversies are about, make your own decisions, and feel more self-assured when expressing your views.

- *It will help you develop concrete, practical communication skills.* These new skills may affect your life in profound ways—shaping your friendships, work, studies, travels, and leisure activities.

- *It will enable you to take action.* While talking is a critical first step, it's clearly not enough. There are numerous ways to become involved in actions that are meaningful to you and that fit your personality and interests.

Finally, this book is not only about survival. We do need to pull together to survive, but we also must join together to make our lives more meaningful and joyful. There are few things that enrich us more or that challenge us and make us think in new ways than encountering people different from ourselves. In a way, then, this is a kit not just for surviving, but for thriving, in a multicultural America.

1

As American as Apple Pie, Tacos, and Egg Rolls

These States are the amplest poem,
Here is not a nation but a teeming Nation
of Nations.

—Walt Whitman

What does it mean to be an American? What is the "American way of life"? Before reading on, imagine that you are a reporter asked to interview a stereotypical, "all-American" family. What type of family would you choose? What do the family members look like? Where do they live? What about their religion? Clothing? Foods?

One possible choice would be the Whitebreads—Mom, Dad, Amber, and Derrick—who live in a spacious house on Crestview Drive with a well-kept lawn, two Japanese cars, and tropical fish. Amber takes oboe and ballet lessons and works summers at a day camp. Derrick (who looks a little like Robert Redford) plays baseball, soccer, and computer games. Mom is an X-ray technician and sings in a church group, and Dad is some type of manager at AT&T and a Little League coach.

If this picture seems too dated to you, reminiscent of the 1950s sitcoms like *Father Knows Best*, you might choose a single-parent family, with either the mother or the father raising the children. Or a childless, two-career couple living in a highrise apartment with a view overlooking the city.

However, my guess is that whatever type of family you would choose—and whatever your own ethnic background might be—certain variables would probably be assumed: a family that represents "America" would be white, middle class, English-speaking, and Christian. And the family members would be able-bodied and heterosexual.

In your interview with the Whitebreads (or their more up-to-date relatives), you would likely learn that they believe in the values that Americans have long cherished: freedom, democracy, equality, hard work, honesty, and self-reliance. They are happy with the "good life"—defined by possessions like a big-screen TV, a microwave, personal computers, and exercise equipment—and they believe that anyone can achieve what they themselves have struggled to obtain. They are proud of this country and find themselves from time to time saying that it is the greatest nation on earth.

For many people, the Whitebreads represent the best in America; it's what we are all about as a nation. This way of life is seen as the goal and standard for millions of Americans, and it has also captured the imagination of people all over the world and inspired generations of immigrants to come here.

But we need to ask some tough questions about all this. Does the family have to be white to be "all-American"? What about an extended Cuban American family living in Little Havana? Or a gay couple? Can the dad qualify if he works as a factory wage earner? Or if he is in a wheelchair?

An anecdote told by Ronald Takaki in his book *A Different Mirror: A History of Multicultural America* provides an example of the deeply ingrained notion that all real Americans are white. On his way to a conference, Takaki chatted with the taxi driver, a white man in his forties.

> "How long have you been in this country?" he asked. "All my life," I replied, wincing. "I was born in the United States." With a strong southern drawl, he remarked, "I was wondering because your English is excellent!" Then, as I had many times before, I explained: "My grandfather came here from Japan in the 1880s. My family has been here, in America, for over a hundred years." He glanced at me in the mirror. Somehow I did not look "American" to him; my eyes and complexion looked foreign.[1]

Similarly, Toni Morrison explains that "deep within the word 'American' is its association with race." For Morrison, "American means white."[2] And Audre Lorde speaks of a "mythical norm" in the United States that is generally defined as "white, thin, male, young, heterosexual, Christian, and financially secure."[3]

At this point in our history we face some fundamental, and uncomfortable, questions about whether the Whitebreads represent who we are,

---

[1] Ronald Takaki, *A Different Mirror: A History of Multicultural America* (Boston: Little, Brown, 1993), 1.

[2] Toni Morrison, *Playing in the Dark: Whiteness in the Literary Imagination* (Cambridge: Harvard University Press, 1992), 47.

[3] Audre Lorde, *Zami/Sister Outsider/Undersong* (Freedom, CA: Crossing Press, 1983), 116.

or who we wish to be. In fact, the inescapable truth about the "all-American" picture we have just sketched is that increasingly large numbers of Americans do not fit it.

Undoubtedly, from the founding of this country onwards, there have been scores of individuals whose lives were dramatically different from the white, Anglo-Saxon, Protestant (WASP) norm. But, somehow, they did not count very much when it came to creating our national identity. One obvious example is the American Indians, who have always been on the margins of society. Since they were not "like us," they have been subjected to a fate of forced removal to reservations and of annihilation. After nearly five hundred years of pressure to conform, many American Indians are still not "like us," and their presence is a forceful reminder that the Whitebreads alone do not define the reality of this country.

As we examine other segments of our population, taking a quick look at demographic statistics, we see that a new picture of who we are needs to be drawn. Consider:

- Already, one in four Americans defines himself or herself as nonwhite or Latino.
- Islam is the fastest-growing religion in America, with an estimated 1,500 houses of worship nationwide.
- One-tenth of the American adult population is estimated to be gay or lesbian.
- As many as forty-five million Americans are estimated to have a physical or mental disability.
- Children speak more than one hundred languages in the school systems of major cities such as New York, Chicago, and Los Angeles.

Nor are the trends represented here expected to reverse themselves. Because of higher birth and immigration rates among nonwhite populations, for example, whites are predicted to be in the minority by about the middle of the twenty-first century. This demographic phenomenon is sometimes referred to as the "browning" of America.

As the country is "browning" and becoming increasingly diverse in other ways, sweeping changes are taking place in nearly every community. In San Jose, California, bearers of the Vietnamese surname Nguyen outnumber the Joneses in the telephone directory four to one. Barbie dolls are now sold in African American, Native American, and Hispanic versions.

J. C. Penney has added a multicultural clothing line to its departments and catalogs, and Hallmark has developed "Mahogany" greeting cards, gift wrap, and accessories to "celebrate African American culture." Salsa has now officially replaced catsup as the top-selling condiment in the country, and bagels have replaced donuts as the most popular breakfast food. People in wheelchairs and on crutches are depicted in commercials for clothes and cars. And ATM machines ask if we would like to read monitor instructions in Spanish or English.

The above examples are relatively nonthreatening; after all, who would mind if the dessert tray now includes baklava as well as apple pie? But the new options, whether welcomed or rejected, are part of a larger, much stormier transformation labeled by the popular press as the "culture wars." In the media, in schools and universities, and in many other contexts in our everyday lives, protracted and often bitter struggles and debates are raging over how to interpret, and adjust to, the extensive changes taking place all around us.

What is at stake in the culture wars, and why should we care? From the point of view of those Americans who have traditionally been in the majority—the Whitebreads—the things they hold sacred are being challenged. These people have long been accustomed to seeing their own faces represented in the national portrait. They know that their ideas and views matter, and they are generally able to make the system work to their own advantage. But now they can easily feel uncertain and threatened. They may be reluctant to welcome others to the table if they fear that the other person's gain will be their loss. And they may find it hard to share what in the past has been exclusively their own.

If this seems a bit too abstract, try to imagine some of the things that now are to be shared. At issue are some of life's most precious opportunities—coveted spaces in prestigious universities as well as in law, medical, and business schools; desirable positions in the trades and the professions; and promotions to higher levels of employment. In addition, to give a few examples on what seems a more mundane level, we are now sharing space on store shelves (with African American hair products), on the airwaves (with Mexican American music), and in our history books (with the heretofore neglected stories of women and minorities). Depending on who you are and what you have come to expect as privileges, you may find that life is getting a bit crowded with the many new competitors.

Not surprisingly, those who have traditionally been excluded from the old gallery of Americans, whether by virtue of race, ethnicity, religion, gender, sexual orientation, age, class, or disability, are impatient to see themselves represented and legitimized as American faces. They are eager to have their piece of the American dream, but—and this is the sticking point for the Whitebreads of society—they may be unwilling to sacrifice their cultural heritage and identity in the process. Rather, they see no reason why they cannot stay basically who they are *and* still be totally "American." Instead of viewing the traditional way of life as a standard, as representative of the people as a whole, they are likely to see it instead as only the "dominant," "mainstream," "Anglo," "Euro-American," or "Eurocentric" culture.

The element of power and control cannot be overlooked. As long as the "other" groups, the nondominant ones, are small and relatively powerless ("marginalized" or "on the fringes"), the dominant culture can generally ignore them. These people, after all, are not the movers and the shakers, they are not part of the national scene, and their ideas and values do not really matter or affect the way decisions are made. They may even be so powerless as to be virtually invisible, as is unforgettably demonstrated by Ralph Ellison in his novel, *The Invisible Man,* when he says: "I am invisible, understand, simply because people refuse to see me." However, when these groups become large or influential enough to assert themselves, then the so-called mainstream interests find themselves challenged in new ways.

The following chapters will discuss the challenges for both groups—those who tend to identify with the more traditional images and those who do not—since both are facing difficult tasks. What lies ahead will test us in ways we have not been tested before as Americans.

7

2

Melting Pot or Salad Bowl?

*America is not like a blanket—one piece
of unbroken cloth, the same color, the
same texture, the same size. America is
more like a quilt—many pieces, many col-
ors, many sizes, all woven and held together by a common thread.*
—The Reverend Jesse Jackson

For generations American society has been described as a melting pot, as one huge, boiling caul-
dron into which all of its people are thrown (or
perhaps they jump in?), and their differences simply melt into a blend.

The "melting pot" metaphor itself was popular-
ized in a play of the same name written by Israel
Zangwill, of Russian Jewish origin, and staged for
the first time in Washington, D.C., in 1908. *The
Melting-Pot* caught on and was performed before
enthusiastic audiences all over the country. Teddy
Roosevelt loved it.

At one point in the play, the main character,
David, cries that America

> is God's crucible, the great Melting-Pot
> where all the races of Europe are melting
> and reforming!... Germans and French-
> men, Irishmen and Englishmen, Jews and
> Russians—into the crucible with you all!
> God is making the American!

The image has stuck in the public's consciousness. It has been referred to countless times in
books, speeches, and the press. It taps into an
idea dear to many Americans: that of *assimila-
tion*. Given our history of mass immigration from
all corners of the earth, it's easy to see why people
believe in the concept.

Basically, newcomers are expected to get rid of
their old identity—their old languages, customs,
and loyalties—as soon as possible and adopt a
new one. They are supposed to blend in, to become like those already here, to become "Ameri-
canized." As Teddy Roosevelt said, the idea of a
"'fifty-fifty' allegiance is impossible in this country: "Either a man is an American and nothing else,
or he is not an American at all."[1]

While the melting pot was supposed to produce
a "new man," because of the country's grounding
in the language, government, religion, and system of laws of England, the basic flavor of the
pot's brew was Anglo-Saxon Protestant. Recall
David's exclamation above that "all the races of
Europe are melting and reforming." No mention
of Africans, Chinese, American Indians, or Mexi-
cans here.

Throughout the twentieth century, critics have
raised objections to the melting pot idea. These

---

[1] Nicolaus Mills, ed., *Arguing Immigration: The Debate over
the Changing Face of America* (New York: Simon and Schuster,
1994), 12.

cultural pluralists have argued for an interpretation of American life that allows and encourages different national and ethnic groups to maintain their distinctiveness and that stresses intergroup cooperation. In a pluralistic society, many different cultures can coexist, all contributing to the whole but not necessarily becoming identical. Until recently, however, the pluralist arguments remained largely unheard.

With increasing interest in multiculturalism, the melting pot theory has undergone serious attack. The critics claim that large segments of the population have simply not melted. Even ardent assimilationists like Arthur Schlesinger, Jr., acknowledge that nonwhite populations—especially African Americans and Native Americans—have generally not melted well, if at all. Furthermore, even among some white groups that were long since thought to have blended in, many people have retained parts of their ethnic and national heritage, and others are beginning to rediscover their past, celebrating a revival of customs, languages, and values.

Now comes a basic question: Is the idea of melting away differences a desirable goal? Are there not many differences worth preserving? What do we end up with after all the simmering is done, and is this the best recipe for building, and preserving, a nation? If not, and if we abandon the melting pot, what do we replace it with? Are we better off, as multiculturalists suggest, with a tossed salad, a mosaic, or a patchwork quilt?

3

Multiculturalism Defined

I am what I am and I am U.S. American
I haven't wanted to say it because if I did
  you'd take away the Puerto Rican but
  now I say go to hell...
I am what I am
I am Puerto Rican
I am U.S. American
I am New York Manhattan and the Bronx
I am what I am
I'm not hiding under no stoop.
                                    —Rosario Morales

The term *multicultural* has entered our daily vocabulary; everywhere we turn, we now hear that
America is a multicultural society. What exactly
does this mean?

The word *multicultural* itself simply means
composed of many cultures, or many distinct
ways of life. By this definition, the United States,
as a nation of immigrants, is inherently
multicultural.

But the philosophy underlying multiculturalism
is more complex. In the 1980s, multiculturalism
became a rallying point for a wide variety of

groups commonly referred to as minorities (sometimes also called "marginalized" groups, "subcultures," or "cocultures") who sought increased recognition and more equal participation in the entire spectrum of American life. Fundamentally opposed to the melting pot theory, these multiculturalists revived the cultural pluralism argument of the early twentieth century, insisting that the American tradition of freedom and democracy should allow them to maintain their unique identities and ways of life.

The phrases commonly used to describe this new movement were often linked to the idea of "celebrating," "valuing," or "affirming" diversity. This was a radical departure from the American past. Now, rather than ignoring, devaluing, or melting away any ethnic or racial departures from the norm, as had been enshrined in both national policy and popular sentiment, Americans were encouraged to see their many differences in cultural background as a source of strength and enrichment. Educators quickly realized that new texts, curricula, and pedagogies would be needed to help students achieve "multicultural awareness" and skills, and the corporate world set about to organize "diversity training" for management and employees.

Who were these multiculturalists, and why did they emerge with such vitality? A large number of them were individuals from different ethnic groups—primarily African, Asian, Hispanic, and Native American—who realized that, despite their differences, they had many goals in common and much to gain by working together (this rather chaotic banding together to form a movement is in evidence throughout this book). Thus, the term *people of color* was born, as nonwhite Americans joined together to formulate common agendas. Their calls for reform were given urgency by huge cuts in social services during the Reagan years, exacerbating persistent problems of poverty, criminality, undereducation, and despair among large segments of the ethnic populations. Additionally, new immigrants from Asia, Mexico, and Central America swelled the numbers of those pressing for change.

What was also significant about the multicultural movement was that it addressed the needs and concerns of minority groups other than those defined by race and ethnicity. Women activists joined the movement, convinced that, even though they were not a numerical minority, they remained marginalized and disempowered in ways similar to the other groups. Gays and lesbians became increasingly visible and vocal as they battled attacks from the religious right and protested the government's passivity in the face of the AIDS epidemic. People with disabilities, whose needs and views had long been ignored, became increasingly active in the burgeoning disability rights movement, culminating in the passage of the Americans with Disabilities Act of 1990.

Multiculturalism thus proved itself to be a flexible, expandable umbrella, capable of encompassing the goals and aspirations of many people outside the mainstream of American life. While some groups and issues tend to appear in the headlines more than others, the less publicized struggles are nonetheless important.

Is there a bottom line, you might ask, or a single unifying principle? On the one hand, the only way to understand the movement is to realize that participation and issues are fluid and constantly changing. If there is a bottom line, then it is human difference—and the discrimination that so often accompanies it. Difference can be based on religion, age, class, gender, ethnicity, national background, sexual orientation, disability, or class—or on other cultural variables. Learning to get along with and respect each other requires that differences (as well as commonalities) be recognized and accepted.

Where is multiculturalism heading? Some opponents suggest that the entire movement is doomed, that it will pass like other fads. If it doesn't simply die off, there's a good chance, some say, that an enormous backlash against it will cause it to go down to defeat. Some thoughtful critics call for a "postethnic America,"[1] in which multiculturalism, inherently flawed by its adherence to an oversimplified grouping of ethnicities into five categories (African American, Asian American, Native American, Latino, and white), will be superseded by a new era of cosmopolitanism based more on categories that are less arbitrary and more flexible.

Multiculturalists themselves, while they might dream of a postethnic society, cannot imagine that the movement will simply fade away or that the issues currently under debate will simply evaporate, especially given the changing demographics in our country. Undoubtedly, however, the central concerns will change and evolve. Some people believe that class issues, still very much a taboo in American society, will emerge as part of a new multicultural agenda. Some predict that children's rights are now just beginning to take their place as a national priority. Whatever the case, the shape

---

[1] See David A. Hollinger, *Postethnic America: Beyond Multiculturalism* (New York: HarperCollins, 1995).

of the multicultural agenda will depend very much on who decides to engage which issues and on how receptive we all are to other people's concerns.

As mentioned in chapter 2, multiculturalists suggest that by respecting each other's concerns and affirming our differences, we can replace the melting pot metaphor with one more suited to the times, such as a tossed salad, mosaic, or patchwork quilt. Jesse Jackson's rainbow coalition also expresses the ideal that we can maintain our uniqueness and yet coexist in a new and harmonious whole.

But is this what is happening? The new metaphors do not explain what occurs if the different parts do not fit together in a pleasing pattern. Thus far, the issues championed by multiculturalists have prompted intense debate in the universities, in the media, and among politicians. The noise has been loud. Culture wars are being waged between the opposing sides. Even among those who consider themselves multiculturalists, there is little agreement on how to proceed on issues of public policy.

The crucial debates—over affirmative action, language, immigration, and related topics—will be discussed in subsequent chapters. Rather than viewing these debates as a problem, an unwanted source of conflict, why not regard them as a necessary, healthy part of life in a multicultural society? As you will see, there is rarely an easy right or wrong position; rather, all the arguments need to be considered and many, weighed carefully. As Gerald Graff eloquently explains in *Beyond the Culture Wars*, what is important for educators is not so much to be an advocate for one position or the other, but to "teach the conflicts."[2] Only then will people understand what is causing the turmoil and be able to make intelligent, informed decisions as to our own positions.

Before we turn to the debates themselves, however, let's take a look at one of the underlying problems in the ongoing cultural conflicts—our tendency to view each other in terms of stereotypes.

---

2 Gerald Graff, *Beyond the Culture Wars: How Teaching the Conflicts Can Revitalize American Education* (New York: W.W. Norton, 1992).

4

Getting beyond Stereotypes

*Americans have no capacity for abstract
thought and make bad coffee.*
—Georges Clemenceau

Cultural stereotypes abound in American society,
and their prevalence reveals how little we really
know about each other. What comes to mind, for
example, when you think of religious groups other
than your own? What images do you have of the
deaf, the blind, or the mentally handicapped?
What do you associate with Arab Americans? Na-
vajos? Appalachians?

Just as an example to see how stereotypes work,
try to think of labels that might be attached to,
say, feminists. Complete the sentence below with
at least five short phrases or adjectives to identify or categorize feminists:

Feminists (are)_____

_____

_____

_____

_____

Some possibilities: bra-burners, braless, man haters, unmarried, unperfumed, humorless, masculine, childless, lesbians, radical, unattractive, intelligent, don't shave their legs, don't wear makeup, hardworking, committed, strident, loud, unreasonable, pushy.

There is some truth to these stereotypes. At a certain point in history, some feminists did burn their bras, and some feminists are lesbians, and some hate men, and some are loud. In fact, stereotypes are usually based on partial truths, but these truths seem always to become so exaggerated and distorted as to be misleading and inaccurate.

Yet one could argue that it is both legitimate and desirable to try to describe and characterize cultural groups. Indeed, the field of anthropology is based on studying and valuing the attributes that distinguish one group from another! We all need some means of organizing information into categories, and there is no way to avoid making generalizations if we wish to talk about, and learn more about, ourselves and our fellow human beings. Not only can the generalizations be illuminating, but they can also promote rather than hinder our understanding of other people.

What do we need to watch out for? How can we distinguish between valid generalizations and unsubstantiated stereotypes? What do we need to understand about how stereotypes work? What makes them dangerous and harmful?

First, we need to recognize that stereotypes tend to be negative, creating fear and raising barriers. If I think, for example, that all Muslims are religious fanatics and terrorists, then why would I want to meet one? If I see all Mexican Americans as lazy, shiftless, uneducated people who are in this country illegally and can't speak English, then I would hardly want to befriend one. Stereotypes keep us apart. They prevent us from learning more about the real people we assign to convenient categories.

Stereotypes also fail to take individual differences into account. We may have never met or spoken with a Mexican American, but we think we know what to expect. Were we to look closer, we would see not only how erroneous, but also how unfair the stereotypes are. What about the many Mexican Americans who work long, strenuous hours in agricultural fields and save money to send home to their families? Are they lazy and shiftless? What about those who are university professors, police officers, teachers, translators, or government officials? Are they uneducated, illegal workers?

Stereotypes are not only unfair to individuals but also to groups within a larger group. When we lump many different peoples together under huge umbrellas like American Indians, we can miss the vast differences between, for example, the Hopi, the Navajo, and the Nez Perce. If we speak of Asian Americans as a whole, do we realize we are including people from more than twenty different countries of origin? Are we aware of the distinctions between those originally from Korea, Japan, China, and the Philippines? What about the differences between Chinese from the mainland, those from Taiwan, and those from Malaysia? Do we have a sense of the various histories, languages, and cultures of recent immigrants from Southeast Asia—Cambodians, Laotians, Vietnamese, and Thais?

Stereotyping affects us all. It's not just a matter of the majority, or the dominant groups, stereotyping the others. Many blacks have stereotypes of Korean Americans, as do Korean Americans of Muslims, and Muslims of Christians. The poor have stereotypes of the rich, as do the rich of the poor. And Korean, Chinese, and Japanese Americans have stereotypes of each other, even though to outsiders they are often thought of as alike.

National surveys confirm that a large percentage of whites as well as minorities tend to believe stereotypes—mostly negative—about each other and, surprisingly, that minorities tend to resent each other almost as much as they do whites. For example, African Americans and Latinos believe that Asian Americans are crafty, unscrupulous, and devious. A majority of nonwhite groups consider whites to be bossy, prejudiced, and unwilling to share power. And nonblack respondents consider African Americans to be lazier, less intelligent, less patriotic, and more violent than whites.

Even so-called positive stereotypes can do harm. Asian Americans, for example, are often seen as the "model minority," excelling in school and the workplace and outpacing their competition. In recent years, however, Asian Americans have begun to protest against this image, recognizing that it not only creates a backlash of resentment but also prevents needed help from reaching many people, such as the Vietnamese and Laotian Americans who are living below the poverty level and clearly not succeeding. Additionally, the positive stereotype can make those who are doing moderately well, but not necessarily winning violin competitions and attending Stanford, feel like failures. And finally, the emphasis on Asian American success can be a disguised way of criticizing African Americans and

Latinos, who, it may be implied, should be more like the superachieving, uncomplaining models from Asia.

Stereotypes do harm in yet another, less understood way when they act as self-fulfilling prophecies. If you hear often enough a stereotyped characterization about a group you are part of, you may eventually come to believe the stereotype and find yourself behaving and thinking accordingly. For example, if girls are not supposed to be good at math, they may not even try to succeed, thus reinforcing the stereotype. If they happen to be proficient and successful at math, they can still end up devoting a great deal of effort to disproving the stereotype, effort that otherwise could be put to better use. Plus, this focus upon dispelling a misconception can produce frustration, erode confidence, and diminish the pleasure and satisfaction of achievement.

African American Claude M. Steele has researched what he calls "stereotype vulnerability." He explains that in the case of a black student, for example, the stereotype that he is less intelligent than others may actually cause him to underachieve on tests. In effect, the student "lives down" to others' expectations of him. Even for those African Americans who do not believe the stereotype, it can become "a threatening hypothesis that they can grow weary of fending off."[1] Steele argues that everyone is subject to stereotype vulnerability in one form or another; a white student, for example, can grow tired of trying to demonstrate that he or she does not conform to the stereotype of the white racist.

---

[1] Claude M. Steele, "Black Students Live Down to Expectations," *New York Times*, 31 August 1995.

Stereotypes can hold up only so long as we see no real people behind them. When we discover each other as actual human beings—with personalities and unique personal stories—we begin to refine our thinking. Once we get to know the various stories of a person or a group, once we have attached names to faces, the fear begins to diminish, and the stereotypes begin to fade.

Practical Suggestions for Dealing with Stereotypes

1. Regard stereotypes with suspicion.
2. Analyze the stereotypes you may have of a group you belong to.
3. Analyze the stereotypes you have of others. Make lists (similar to the feminist list) and try to be as honest as possible in confronting your own stereotypes.
4. Test stereotypes against your own information and experiences.
5. Always be prepared to discard your stereotypes and to revise and refine generalizations about groups of people.
6. Analyze your language for stereotypes that unwittingly creep in: using the expression "to jew someone down" for trying to get a lower price; "Indian giver" for someone who goes back on her word; to "gyp" (from Gypsy), meaning to cheat; and "yellow bellied" to indicate cowardliness.
7. When talking about groups of people, use qualifying words like *generally, tend to, often, likely to be.*

8. When you discover "exceptions to the rule," be prepared to revise the rule rather than simply declare an exception.

9. Try to discover what the stereotypes you hear or hold are based on.

10. Be on the lookout for reinforcement of stereotypes in Hollywood and the media (all African American mothers are single and on welfare, all Asian American women are seductive).

11. Talk with friends or acquaintances about their views on how they are stereotyped and about their stereotypes of you.

12. Don't expect your stereotypes of yourself or others to change overnight; this is a lifelong process.

5

The Ugly America: Hate Groups and Hate Crimes

> Remember, to hate, to be violent, is demeaning. It means you're afraid of the other side of the coin—to love and be loved.
>
> —James Baldwin

When negative stereotypes are rigidly applied, stigmatizing and dehumanizing entire groups of people, violence in the form of hate crimes is never far away. This is the ugly side of life in a multicultural society. We are all familiar with the shameful stories throughout our history of entire groups that have been oppressed, interned, enslaved, or annihilated, and we know as well that these chapters of the American past provide the backdrop for countless tales of individual persecution.

Before attempting to look at the current situation, let's clarify that hate crimes (also called "bias crimes") are acts of intimidation or violence directed at individuals or groups, most commonly but not exclusively because of their race, ethnicity, religion, or sexual orientation. Some feminist researchers and groups, including the National Organization for Women (NOW), argue that violent crimes against women—crimes motivated by misogyny—should also be considered hate crimes, a position which causes not only a drastic rethinking of the concept but also a huge increase in the number of people affected.

Hate crimes are considered to be especially dangerous, since they affect not only the individual victim (or victims) but also the entire group to which the victim belongs. When a gay man is beaten up, a synagogue vandalized, or the door of a black student's dormitory room defaced, the action in question sends a message to the victim's entire community that its members are not safe, not wanted, at risk. Recognizing the unique severity of hate crimes, the United States Supreme Court upheld in 1993 a Wisconsin state law that allowed enhanced penalties for hate crimes (such as longer prison sentences for persons convicted). Almost all the states, and some cities, currently have hate crime laws. These laws generally punish crimes that victimize people because of their race, ethnicity, or religion. Some also include sexual orientation, disability, age, and gender.

What motivates hate crimes? Social scientists have long studied the roots of prejudice and violence, and, should you be interested, you can find a wealth of literature on this topic. The classic study remains *The Nature of Prejudice* by Gordon Allport, and many other scholars have attempted to shed light on the topic of prejudice, though comparatively little research has been done specifically into the nature of hate crimes.

There is an enormous range of hate crimes, from threatening phone calls and street harassment, to arson and vandalism, to rape and murder. The perpetrators can be gangs of teenage offenders seeking a thrill, lone offenders protecting their communities from outsiders, or "true believers" who dedicate their lives to their mission.[1]

Any of the offenders, but particularly the "true believers," might be members of hate groups (usually, but not always, synonymous with white supremacist organizations). Klanwatch, one of several organizations that monitor hate crimes nationwide, estimates that 350 hate organizations are currently active throughout the country, with an estimated membership of twenty-five thousand hard-core adherents and hundreds of thousands of sympathizers. What the groups have in common is a fundamental belief in white supremacy and male domination, combined with profound antisemitism and homophobia.

Historically, the Ku Klux Klan (KKK) has been at the core of the movement. For over one hundred years it has been associated with intimidation and organized terror, creating powerful symbols of white-hooded riders and nightly cross burnings. (Actually, the Klan is not a single organization, but a conglomeration of groups, each of which has the word *Klan* in its title, such as the White Knights of the KKK.)

The KKK today has many fewer members than it did earlier in the century, due in part to the growth of other similar competing groups. The Christian Identity Movement, which believes that

---

[1] See Jack Levin and Jack McDevitt, *Hate Crimes: The Rising Tide of Bigotry and Bloodshed* (New York: Plenum Press, 1993).

white Anglo-Saxons are God's only true children and that Jews are descended from Satan, uses religion to justify bigotry. Neo-Nazi organizations subscribe to Hitler's ideology and practice extreme forms of antisemitism. Closely related, Neo-Nazi Skinhead groups, which emerged in the early 1980s, exist as youth gangs in urban areas. This fast-growing young generation of racists, distinguished at first by shaved heads, swastika tattoos, and steel-toed boots, has proven itself to be the most brutally violent group of white supremacists to have emerged in recent decades.

Some experts believe that the most dangerous white supremacists have now moved into the so-called "Patriot" movement, a broad coalition of right-wing antigovernment extremists. Within the past decade, these militia bands, united in their hatred of and the intent by many of them to destroy the government by armed revolt, have grown to include an estimated twelve million adherents, and more than four hundred armed militias have been identified throughout the country. While the Patriots' antigovernment agenda includes militant stances against abortion and environmentalism as well as ardent gun support, the overlap with white supremacist ideology is extensive.

Whether acting as Patriots, as members of other hate groups, or as lone individuals, extremists and white supremacists now have a powerful new tool at their disposal: the Internet. The explosive growth of a computer hate network over the past few years, with colorful, sophisticated "home pages" and a variety of "newsgroups," has led to the coining of a new term: *cyberhate*. The advantage of the Internet is its speed, worldwide access, and low cost.

What actually is being done to counter the activities of hate groups? On a federal level, the major agency charged with investigating, monitoring, and prosecuting hate crime offenders is the Federal Bureau of Investigation (FBI). In addition, as mentioned above, many states and some cities have enacted some form of antibias legislation. Private advocacy groups such as the Southern Poverty Law Center (which operates Klanwatch), the Center for Democratic Renewal (CDR), the Anti-Defamation League of B'nai B'rith (ADL), the National Gay and Lesbian Task Force (NGLTF), and the Women's Project are working to combat bigotry through monitoring, litigation, and education.

Worthy of special mention is the Southern Poverty Law Center's remarkable record of success in bringing civil lawsuits against the nation's most powerful racist organizations. With a brilliant strategy designed to make the organization itself and its leaders liable for crimes of its followers, the Center has won landmark cases, including multimillion dollar verdicts in nationally publicized murder cases against the United Klans of America and the White Aryan Resistance (WAR) group, virtually bankrupting the two offending organizations.

Why, ultimately, is it important to learn about hate groups and bias crimes? The most important, and provocative, reason is offered by Raphael S. Ezekiel in *The Racist Mind: Portraits of American Neo-Nazis and Klansmen*. An American Jew deeply opposed to racist ideology, Ezekiel spent a decade interviewing white supremacists and their followers, observing their meetings and rallies, and reading their literature. He suggests that all of America is implicated in the racism, sexism, and homophobia that we see in extremist groups. In other words, just by virtue of the fact that we have grown up in America, each one of us has absorbed—even if we wish it were not so—some of the thinking that results in discrimination and violence. We can better understand who we are by becoming more familiar with the "racist mind" of radicals, since we share, in a less exaggerated form, the same types of biases that prompt their antisocial behavior. Militant white supremacists, Ezekiel says, allow us to "see the racist parts of our souls with few filters; we should observe and learn."[2]

Ezekiel reminds us that bigotry is found everywhere, and sometimes in unexpected places. Just as African Americans and Jews can be homophobic, gays can be racist and the disabled can be antisemitic. One's own oppression does not always make for more sensitivity to, or solidarity with, other oppressed people or groups.

You might wish to take some time to think about your own life and your personal situation. How tolerant do you consider your family to be? If you are a parent (or plan to be), how are you raising your children? If you are a student, what about the atmosphere at your school? (Many schools and college campuses have experienced bitter racial, antisemitic, and antigay incidents in the past decade.) What about your own town or neighborhood? How integrated is it? How are gays and lesbians, the elderly, and the homeless treated? (See chapter 20 for a discussion of how local citizens responded to hate crimes in a Montana town.) Your

---

[2] Raphael S. Ezekiel, *The Racist Mind: Portraits of American Neo-Nazis and Klansmen* (New York: Penguin, 1995), 323.

response to these questions can help you understand the role we all play in either creating or discouraging the conditions for hate.

6

What's in a Name?: Speech Codes and Retreats into Silence

Sticks and stones can break my bones, but names can never harm me.
                              —Children's rhyme

Where do we draw the line, you might ask, between hate crimes and hate speech? Are people free to say and print whatever they please about others, no matter how offensive, demeaning, or hostile? Is hate speech protected by the First Amendment?

Many multiculturalists believe that hate speech must be prohibited by law. Some take the approach that speaking in itself is an action—that words are deeds—and can be punished as such. Other advocates of legal restrictions use the concept of "fighting words" to explain why certain insults, slurs, epithets, and derogatory language cannot be seen as "only words," but in fact are so inflammatory and harmful as to be a first act of aggression equivalent to a physical blow. Still others use the concept of a "hostile environment" to explain why hate speech cannot be tolerated. Whatever their reasoning, these advocates point out that the guarantee of free speech has never been absolute; the courts have allowed for dozens of exceptions, including libel, plagiarism, fraud, perjury, invasion of privacy, obscenity, and speech that creates a clear and present danger (such as shouting "fire" in a crowded theater). Hate speech, restrictionists argue, should simply be one more exception.

Yet the overriding sentiment in this country says otherwise and protects hate speech—which includes nonverbal communication such as armbands, flags, symbols, pictures, parades, and insignia—under the First Amendment. Defenders of First Amendment rights often use the "slippery slope" argument, claiming that once one begins to limit some speech, then restrictions will keep increasing until we have full-blown repression.

How, for example, do you decide which groups to protect? Should only the historically disadvantaged ethnic, religious, racial, and national groups be protected, or should anyone be protected from insult, including the dominant group? ("He's a male chauvinist, capitalist pig.") Should derogatory labels such as "white trash" be outlawed? How about other types of verbal affronts? ("You're just an overstudious computer nerd!") Will we end up censoring art and taking books off the shelves because somebody, somewhere, is offended? As African American Congresswoman Eleanor Holmes Norton explains, "It is technically impossible to write an antispeech code that cannot be twisted against speech nobody means to bar. It has been tried and tried and tried."[1]

Moreover, how does one determine whether something is truly offensive? Words take their meaning from context, and who is to say later in court whether a comment was made to harm or in jest? And let's not forget, free speech defenders say, that the meaning of a word changes, depending on when it is used and who uses it. Previously neutral terms, like *colored people* or *Negro*, may become outdated and, to many, unacceptable. A highly charged word like *nigger* might be easily identifiable as an insult, but what if African Americans themselves use it, as in the rap group NWA—short for "Niggas with Attitude"? (See chapter 19 for a related case study dealing with the limits of humor.)

Even if certain language is deemed to be highly offensive, free speech advocates believe it must be confronted in the "marketplace of ideas" rather than stifled. This is the "speech you hate" argument; the more you detest the speech, the greater the obligation to protect it.

In light of the reluctance shown to pass legislation in the United States, you may be surprised to learn that many other countries of the world have taken decisive steps to ban hate speech and outlaw the dissemination of hateful racial or religious propaganda. In Germany, for example, the government has banned a number of extremist groups, outlawed Nazi emblems, and made it illegal to deny the Holocaust. Also, key interna-

---

[1] Ira Glasser, "Introduction," in *Speaking of Race, Speaking of Sex*, by Henry Louis Gates, Jr., Anthony P. Griffin, Donald E. Lively, Robert C. Post, William B. Rubenstein, and Nadine Strossen (New York: New York University Press, 1994), 4.

tional human rights declarations, such as the 1965 International Convention on the Elimination of All Forms of Racial Discrimination, prohibit racial and religious propaganda. This United Nations Convention, ratified by more than 130 countries, has not been ratified by the United States.

In this country the most serious, active efforts to restrict hate speech have taken place on college and university campuses. In response to a shocking epidemic of bias incidents on campuses in the 1980s and 1990s—ranging from malicious spoofs to violent attacks—vocal minority students and faculty, determined to protect their rights, have set in motion a speech code movement that has subsequently swept colleges and universities. Typical of the hundreds of codes of conduct restricting offensive speech was the University of Michigan policy, which prohibited "any behavior, verbal or physical, that stigmatizes or victimizes an individual on the basis of race, ethnicity, religion, sex, sexual orientation, creed, national origin, ancestry, age, marital status, handicap, or Vietnam-era veteran status."

In defense of such restrictions on speech, some of the finest legal scholars in the country have put forth provocative new challenges to the First Amendment. An entire body of literature has evolved, much of which pits the Fourteenth Amendment's guarantees of equal protection under the law to all citizens against traditional First Amendment rights. As feminist scholar Catherine MacKinnon succinctly states, "The law of equality and the law of freedom of speech are on a collision course in this country."[2]

---

[2] Catherine MacKinnon, *Only Words* (Cambridge: Harvard University Press, 1993), 71.

Understanding what the new challenge means is difficult, since most of us have been raised to revere the First Amendment, regarding any threat to it as a danger to our very liberty, cherishing it as a safeguard to our right to dissent, and, basically, not questioning it. Groundbreaking arguments have come from MacKinnon, whose *Only Words* is widely cited, and from "minority" law professors Mari J. Matsuda, Charles R. Lawrence III, Richard Delgado, and Kimberlè Williams Crenshaw, whose work appears in *Words That Wound: Critical Race Theory, Assaultive Speech and the First Amendment.* According to these scholars, hate speech violates the law of equality because it acts to subordinate women and minorities. Through fear and intimidation, it keeps people in their place, maintains their status as second-class citizens, and denies them the benefits of full access to public life and services.

The hate speech issue is, as one scholar put it, "the hardest free speech question of all."[3] It has not only created a virulent backlash; it has also divided many traditional supporters of civil rights and civil liberties—members of groups such as the American Civil Liberties Union (ACLU) and the American Association of University Professors (AAUP)—into opposing camps. In the first court challenges, including a 1992 Supreme Court decision, speech codes were struck down as violations of First Amendment rights. But the issues have not been put to rest, and the debates continue.

As these controversies over whether we have a right to use certain kinds of language swirl about

---

[3] Rodney Smolla, *Free Speech in an Open Society* (New York: Alfred A. Knopf, 1992), 151.

us, filling volumes of legal journals and taking their circuitous route through the court system, most of us carry on with our everyday lives. Are we affected by the furor over language? While we may not understand the fine points of law, we are probably sensing a mood of uncertainty and tension that has crept into our daily speech. We now worry not only about what is *legal*, but about what is *acceptable* or *appropriate* speech.

Putting aside First Amendment issues for a moment, let's assume that—whether punishable by law or not—most of us simply do not *want* to use insulting or hostile language. Contrary to the nursery rhyme quoted at the opening of this chapter, we know that language can cause harm, and we consciously avoid words and phrases that would fall into the category of slurs, insults, or epithets.

Sometimes, however, language contains cultural slights or insults that may not be apparent. How can we learn to detect the subtleties of insensitive language? For example, let's say we've heard that certain words are "in," and others are "out," but we're not sure which to use. Henry Louis Gates, Jr., tells us that he began his application for admission to Yale University in 1968 with the sentence: "My grandfather was colored, my father is Negro, and I am black."[4] To which he might add today, "and my son is African American, or a person of color." Why are there so many changes, and how do we keep track of them? Furthermore, do they really matter?

From the multiculturalists' point of view, they do matter. Since language not only reveals, but

---

[4] Henry Louis Gates, Jr., *Loose Canons: Notes on the Culture Wars* (New York: Oxford University Press, 1992), 134.

also shapes, the way we think about ourselves and others, shadings and subtleties can become very important. In many cases it may simply be important to use certain language because a person or group prefers it. Immigrants from Latin America, for example, may reject the term *Hispanic* because it recalls the colonization by Spain. Members of certain ethnic and cultural groups may dislike the term *minority* because it suggests "lesser." As such designations continue to change, this evolution may cause inconvenience for the outsider, but it may be deemed necessary and appropriate by the people directly affected. The process of defining one's identity involves changes, and what was good for one group at one time may not be for the next.

But the issue of culturally insensitive language is much more far-reaching than naming and labeling. Often, biases are embedded in the structure and vocabulary of the English language itself. Toward the goal of "bias-free," "nonsexist," or "inclusive" language, multiculturalists see the need to make some fundamental changes in the ways in which we speak and write. For example, many women object to the way *man* functions as a generic term in English (as in *mankind, chairman, layman, freshman, man-made, manpower*). Similarly, the idea that *black* is negative or evil is built into the English language: *blackmail, blackball, black marks* (on your record), *black market, blackhearted, blacklist, black sheep*. Such biases prove difficult to eliminate.

To help people keep track of the widely accepted and newly proposed changes in language, guides to bias-free language are being distributed in schools and the workplace and sold in bookstores. And dictionaries are being revised to include new vocabulary and definitions as well as to warn when words are offensive or disparaging.

You can be sure that the many changes in our language are not going unchallenged. Some people do not appreciate the new labels, viewing them as euphemisms that are inaccurate and untruthful, serving only to debase and unnecessarily complicate the language. They object, for example, to replacing *disabled* or *handicapped* with *differently abled* or *physically challenged*. Are there no deficiencies, anymore, they wonder, or is everything to be seen as a special or different ability?

These critics make endless fun of what they view as the hypersensitivity to language. Where does it end, they ask? Does a man-eating shark have to be called a "person-eating shark"? Are the homeless simply "people with special housing needs"? Are corpses "organically challenged"?

On a more serious note, the critics of multiculturalism wonder who has the right to make up, and insist on, all these new rules. While their charges that "language police" are out patrolling is overstated, they do seem justified in asking how these decisions regarding changes are getting made. One possible rule, as discussed above, is to respect the wishes of the people most directly affected, but, in truth, there is rarely consensus even in the groups themselves. Some folks of advanced age like the term *senior citizens*; some prefer *elderly;* and some don't seem to mind just being *old*. Some women like *Ms.*, while others prefer *Miss* or *Mrs.* Of course, when critics ask who has the right to make up the new rules, they cannot avoid being asked in return who had the right to make up the prevailing ones.

The unintended and potentially disastrous effect of implementing speech codes and promoting language reform is that the resulting confusion, and fear of making a mistake, can produce silence. Well-meaning people can be so worried about saying the wrong thing—and thus being thought of as insensitive, uninformed, racist, or sexist—that they say nothing (see chapter 13 on PC). The very topics, then, that are most in need of discussion get avoided, and the questions that most need to be asked get self-censored.

There is no easy way out of this dilemma. You might take a moment to think about times when you have been silenced and consider how you might have reacted differently. There is no denying the risks of speaking out, but aren't the risks of *not* speaking much greater? Cornel West says that the absence of candid, critical public dialogue about race leaves us "intellectually debilitated, morally disempowered and personally depressed."[5] If we do not wish to succumb to the paralysis around us, we will need to learn new "languages"—new ways of engaging each other in genuine dialogue.

Practical Suggestions for Language Use

1. Try to learn what is "in" and what is "out"—and the reasons—but don't get hung up. Unless you're using an outright slur, your indiscretion will probably not be grave (assuming you're not a politician). Besides, nobody agrees on the fine points anyway, and the "rules" keep changing.

---

[5] Cornel West, "Learning to Talk of Race," *New York Times Magazine*, 2 August 1992.

2. If you get stuck in conversation, admit that you don't know what to say. Maybe someone can help you.

3. If you don't know how to refer to someone from an ethnic, religious, or other group, ask him or her directly and politely.

4. If you make a "mistake" and someone corrects you, don't be offended. Simply thank the person and carry on.

5. Keep your sense of humor, especially when you blunder. Be prepared to laugh at yourself.

6. If someone refers to you using terminology you don't appreciate (such as *Oriental*, which suggests exoticism), try to be gentle. Rising up in outrage will only make the situation worse.

7. Take words seriously, but not too seriously. People tend to be forgiving if they know you're making an effort. Besides, experts estimate that 60-90 percent of what we communicate is nonverbal, so your meaning may be understood even if your words are awkward or mischosen.

8. Remember that the context matters more than the words themselves. (Your eighty-year-old white grandmother, who has been in a nursing home for years, may still use the word *Negro*, but she may use it more respectfully than a bigot who talks disparagingly about African Americans.)

9. Let people know you're not interested in hearing language or jokes that demean others.

10. Practice using new terms and new language. You may be uncomfortable at first, but soon you'll feel more natural.

7

Cultural vs. Multicultural Literacy: The Canon Debate

When someone with the authority of a teacher...describes the world and you are not in it, there is a moment of psychic disequilibrium, as if you looked into a mirror and saw nothing.
—Adrienne Rich

Have you ever asked yourself what kinds of things you need to know as an American? Imagine, for example, that you're teaching a class for a group of newly arrived immigrants from all over the world. What would you want them to learn about their new country? Or suppose you're on the school board for your children's elementary school. What should the children study in order to become educated Americans? What books should they read? What kinds of things should they be tested on?

While these types of questions are as old as

education itself, a new version of the debate was touched off in the late 1980s by two professors, Allan Bloom and E. D. Hirsch, Jr. Their books, *The Closing of the American Mind* and *Cultural Literacy: What Every American Needs to Know*, became national best-sellers, and the authors received enormous media attention.

What alarmed Bloom, Hirsch, and many others is what they saw as widespread ignorance and illiteracy in the country. Horror stories abounded: according to various surveys, large percentages of high school seniors were unable to identify the author of *Moby Dick*, say anything meaningful about Thomas Jefferson, or place the Civil War in the correct century. When asked about Hoover, all they could think of was a dam or a vacuum cleaner.

The remedy, according to Hirsch, is to reclaim the body of knowledge that we all have in common: our shared heritage. Without that unifying knowledge, Hirsch believes, things deteriorate into chaos and confusion. He calls that body of background information "cultural literacy," and the appendix to his book contains, as the front cover states, a list of "5,000 essential names, phrases, dates, and concepts."

To test your own cultural literacy, see how many of the following sample entries from the *H* section of Hirsch's sixty-three-page appendix, "What Literate Americans Know,"[1] you can identify:

H_2O	Hannibal
habeas corpus	Hanoi
habitat	Hansel and Gretel (title)

---

[1] E. D. Hirsch, Jr., *Cultural Literacy: What Every American Needs to Know* (New York: Random House, 1987), 176.

H-bomb

Hades

Had we but world
  enough, and time...

Hague, The

Hail-fellow-well-met

hairsplitting

Haiti

Hale, Nathan

Half a loaf is
  better than none

half-life

hallucination

Hamburg

Hamilton, Alexander

Hamlet (title)

hammer and sickle

Hancock, John

Handel

handwriting
  on the wall, the

Hanukkah

hara-kiri

Harding, Warren G.

hard water

hardwired

Hare and the Tortoise,
  The (title)

Harlem, NY

Harpers Ferry

harpsichord

harpy

Hartford, CT

Haste makes waste

Hastings, Battle of

Havana

Hawaii

hawks and doves

Haydn, Joseph

hearsay

Hearst, William Randolph

If you have a chance, glance through the complete list at the back of Hirsch's book, or take a look at his *Dictionary of Cultural Literacy.* Do you think this type of shared knowledge is the glue that holds us together as a society? Has Hirsch captured the essence of American culture and society?

As you might suspect, multiculturalists do not think so. A response to Hirsch and Bloom, entitled *Multicultural Literacy: Opening the American Mind*, appeared in 1988. The editors, Rick Simonson and Scott Walker, consider much of the Hirsch/Bloom worldview to be outdated, and they "take issue with Hirsch's and Bloom's definitions of what (or whose) culture should be taught."[2] They are distressed by what the list leaves out. So, the editors have appended their own list to the anthology, providing an alternative to Hirsch's "particular white, male, academic, eastern U.S., Eurocentric bias."[3] Their *H* section includes the following entries omitted by Hirsch:

Haida (tribe)	Hebrew
Hall, Radclyffe	Hell
Halloween	Hidalgo, Miguel
Hamburger Hill	History is bunk
Hamilton, Edith	Holiday, Billie
Hansberry, Lorraine (Raisin in the Sun)	homeopathy
	homophobia
Happy Birthday (song)	Hopi
Harlem Renaissance	hostile takeover
Hasidic	Hughes, Langston
Health Maintenance Organization	Hurston, Zora Neale
	Hydra
Heaney, Seamus	hyperspace
Heaven	hysterectomy

If you find yourself getting irritated or puzzled over either of the lists (Why do I need to know about the Battle of Hastings or the Hopi? And who says I do? How much do I need to know?), you're beginning to feel the heat of the "canon wars" being fought on the "battleground of the curriculum."

The canon is no more than the "must-reads," the accumulated writings that are considered es-

---

2 Rick Simonson and Scott Walker, eds., *The Graywolf Annual 5: Multicultural Literacy, Opening the American Mind* (Saint Paul, MN: Graywolf Press, 1988), x.

3 Ibid., xii.

sential for a basic education. Used within the church to refer to the officially approved code of law (canon law) and to the officially recognized books of the Bible (biblical canon), the word refers more generally to an authoritative list of works. Whether you knew it or not, you were plowing through the literary canon in high school English when you read Shakespeare, Jane Austen, Steinbeck, and Hemingway. These are the classic texts—the ones that, so the theory goes, any educated person needs to be familiar with and that, therefore, are assigned over and over again in classrooms.

There are canons everywhere, not only in literature, but in music, history, art, and religion. Usually we're not even aware that they exist because they seem to be so natural—they appear to be givens. Who, for example, would deny that Mozart, Beethoven, Bach, and Brahms belong to the musical canon with which Americans ought to be familiar? But contrary to what we might think at first about the obvious nature of canons, the truth is that they are always in dispute, and always changing. Consider your favorite musician. How does he or she get included among the "greats" (and then studied in schools)? What are the criteria? Who makes the decisions? Should the Beatles be included? Elton John? Ella Fitzgerald? What about music from Ghana? From India?

Hirsch's plea for cultural literacy is a defense of the traditional, classical canon, as is former Secretary of Education William Bennett's call for a return to the "basics" in education. Along the same lines, some educators, like Bloom, defend the *Great Books of the Western World*, a collection of fifty-four volumes published by Encyclopedia Britannica that contains the texts considered to be the foundation of our culture (Homer, Plato, Shakespeare, Kant, Marx, Freud, and so on). The *Great Books* volumes reflect the traditionalists' tendency to focus on Western culture and heritage and draw heavily on Europe as the fount of civilization. A 1990 revised edition, the first since the original publication in 1952, added four women, but no blacks, to the 130 authors represented. Expressing disappointment that not even W. E. B. Du Bois was included, Henry Louis Gates, Jr., concludes, "Obviously, there's still a 'whites only' sign on what precisely constitutes a great thinker."[4]

For many multiculturalists, the problem with the traditional canons is that they see themselves left out. Where are the great women writers, artists, and thinkers, they ask? Where are African Americans and Native Americans? Why should we study only DWEMs (Dead White European Males)? Why only learn about the traditions that lead back to Europe? After all, the heritage of African Americans, Asian Americans, and Latinos is traced to other continents. Many minority group members feel that the standard curricula and texts impose values from the dominant society on them, while disregarding their own lives and history.

It is not easy for those who have always been represented in the canon to understand what this disregard means. Being excluded can have a profound emotional effect. The message is that you are a nobody. Year after year of getting this message in school can result in feelings of inferiority and alienation, as expressed in the chapter opening quotation by Adrienne Rich.

---

[4] Edwin McDowell, "Books by Women Are Added to Canon," *New York Times*, 25 October 1990.

The struggle over the canon is changing the face of education from preschool to the university. There is now a flourishing multicultural literature for children, ranging from Hmong and Navajo folktales to depictions of families with two mommies to stories of children with disabilities. Entire curricula for school systems have been revised, and basic textbooks read by millions of schoolchildren have been rewritten amidst furious controversies involving teachers, parents, civic leaders, and specialists. In the universities, advocates of ethnic studies, African American studies, women's studies, and Chicano studies are all challenging the traditional canon. Scholars like Molefi Kete Asante, professor of African American Studies at Temple University, are calling for an "Afrocentric" curriculum (see page 59).

Perhaps the most widely publicized expression of the battles over curriculum was the 1988 demonstration at Stanford University, at which Jesse Jackson and about five hundred students chanted, "Hey hey, ho ho, Western culture's got to go." While critics sometimes cite this and similar dramatic stories to frighten people, there was never any danger of Western culture being overthrown. Revisions were made in Stanford's core curriculum and certain readings were added, but the study of Western culture is still very much intact there, as elsewhere.

Though tumultuous, this is a very exciting time for education. Questions of great importance are being asked about what it is that we want, or need, to learn about ourselves. Fascinating new research by multiculturalists is proving that there is a wealth of previously unknown material out there and that DWEMs are not the only valid subject for study.

What we are beginning to understand is that it is not a question of "the" canon or "their" canon, but "our" canon. Every one of us has a stake in deciding what is read and taught, and what type of literacy we wish to achieve. We need to be aware of the debates and to be part of them. Furthermore, we need to remember that it is not only a matter of what is read and what is taught, but how it is taught. This is the focus of the next chapter.

8

New Voices:
Rewriting Our History

Until the lion writes his own story, the tale
of the hunt will always glorify the hunter.
—African proverb

The year 1992—the five-hundredth anniversary of Christopher Columbus's journey to the New World—gave us an unprecedented opportunity for a history lesson. What originally was planned as a massive celebration of the explorer's noble stature and worthy accomplishments turned instead into an equally massive debate on who Columbus really was—a hero or a villain. Was he a man of vision and daring, a brave adventurer and consummate mariner to whom we owe our everlasting tribute for opening up this vast continent? Or was he a greedy, unscrupulous fortune hunter who, concerned only for his own wealth and reputation, was responsible for the destruction of the land as well as unspeakable crimes against indigenous populations in the New World and in Africa?

Survival Kit for Multicultural Living

As the controversy continued unabated for several years leading up to the events of 1992, many plans for Columbus-friendly parades, exhibitions, and projects were canceled, including the United Nations celebration, and some were replaced by anti-Columbus demonstrations and presentations. A new, radically different interpretation of Columbus was emerging, one that had little in common with what was written in the history books. Even the language used to talk about Columbus became a topic of dispute; the famous "discovery" of the "new world" was, at best, an "encounter" and, at worst, a "conquest" or "invasion."

Why, all of a sudden, was the familiar Columbus story no longer being retold as usual? What happened was that passionate new voices with new opinions were brought forth. Indigenous people throughout the Americas, people who had suffered as a result of Columbus's deeds, were no longer willing to be silent. They organized conferences, undertook speaking tours, and wrote articles. Some of their efforts are documented in the film *Columbus Didn't Discover Us.*[1] For the first time, the views expressed by these new voices on Columbus were brought into the public consciousness.

You will likely encounter this metaphor of "voice" again and again in multicultural studies. Though used in the past, its renewed popularity is owed in large part to the influence of feminism. A groundbreaking book by Carol Gilligan, *In a Different Voice: Psychological Theory and Women's Development* (1982), supports the idea that women's expressions of their self-concept and

---

[1] This video is available from Turning Tide Productions (tel. 508-544-8313).

56

moral views, while different from men's, are nevertheless valid. Women's different "voice" needs to be heard, Gilligan says, rather than be repressed or silenced.

This powerful image of new voices speaking out—and being listened to—captures the spirit of multiculturalism. Historians, in particular, are faced with no less than a full-scale reexamination and revision of standard accounts of the past (thus the term *revisionist* history). Whose history matters? That of conquerors, presidents, and military leaders? That of people like us? That of women, children, workers, or slaves? And who is entitled to tell history?

From a Native American perspective, for example, not only Columbus, but the entire panorama of U.S. history, look quite different from what most of us learned (or are learning) in school and have come to accept as orthodox. The establishment of the original settlements along the Eastern seaboard is seen not as the story of endurance and survival against all odds—a great triumph remembered and celebrated each year with a feast in November—but rather as a tale of betrayal, mistreatment, and theft. In his essay *For Indians, No Thanksgiving*, Michael Dorris explains that the holiday does not have the same meaning for Native Americans as for others; it is a time of grief rather than of giving thanks.[2]

Similarly, the story of the westward expansion—an epic of adventure and bravery that fulfilled a great "destiny" for those pioneers conquering new frontiers—becomes instead an epic of destruction, greed, and violation. Dee Brown's *Bury My Heart*

---

[2] Michael Dorris, *Paper Trail: Essays* (New York: HarperCollins, 1994), 228-31.

at Wounded Knee: An Indian History of the American West gives full attention to events, names, and places that might otherwise receive cursory treatment, or be ignored entirely. The title of the book, which places at the center an event relatively unknown and unimportant to non-Indians, already lets us know that this is not the version of history normally told.

If you are interested in multicultural or revisionist history, you might begin with Dee Brown's book or with Ronald Takaki's *Strangers from a Different Shore: A History of Asian Americans* or his *A Different Mirror: A History of Multicultural America*; Howard Zinn's *A People's History of the United States*; or Bonnie S. Anderson and Judith P. Zinsser's two-volume *A History of Their Own: Women in Europe*.

Part of the joy of reading these histories is seeing how new sources of information are tapped. Dee Brown explains that while the great myths of the American West were being created, "only occasionally was the voice of an Indian heard." Yet, he says, "they are not all lost, those Indian voices of the past."[3] Some accounts can be found in pictographs; in speeches translated into English; or in obscure journals, pamphlets, and books. Records of treaty councils contain first-person statements by Indians, as do some newspaper interviews. From almost forgotten sources, Brown has tried to describe the Indians' experiences, based on their own firsthand accounts.

This type of multicultural or revisionist history is not universally acclaimed. Predictably, some

---

[3] Dee Brown, *Bury My Heart at Wounded Knee: An Indian History of the American West* (New York: Henry Holt, 1970), xvii.

of the established voices feel threatened by the challenges to their views. And since these voices tend to have power and money, they continue to control much of what becomes public. During the Columbus quincentennial, for example, critics accused the National Endowment for the Humanities (NEH) of bias in rejecting proposals that took a less than favorable view of Columbus. Of these, the most ambitious—a four-part television miniseries titled "1492: Clash of Visions"—was denied a $500,000 NEH grant, even though the series had been supported by the agency's own advisory council of prominent historians. The producer, whose intent was to portray the indigenous empires that flourished at the time of Columbus's landings, was informed that the rejection was due to the project's "lack of evenhandedness."[4]

The question of who controls history—and how the criteria for historical validity are established—is illustrated most vividly by recent bitter controversies over "Afrocentrism." On the one hand, revisionists like Martin Bernal, author of *Black Athena*, and Molefi Kete Asante are calling for an Afrocentric curriculum, which would allow students to learn more about Africa, Africans, and African Americans than is the case with the current Eurocentric emphasis. Afrocentric scholars generally regard ancient Egypt as the source of Western civilization, rather than Greece. Their arguments hinge on claims that Egypt was a black civilization, and that Greece owed much of its philosophy and scientific thought to Egypt.

In opposition to these views, classical scholar Mary Lefkowitz, author of *Not out of Africa: How*

---

[4] Stephan Salisbury, "Critics Claim Head of NEH Shows Bias," *Oregonian*, 20 June 1991.

Afrocentrism Became an Excuse to Teach Myth as History, characterizes Afrocentrism as a myth for which there is no historical evidence. Though charged with being a racist, she insists that she is simply defending the idea that history must be based on truths, not on inventions. Other critics of Afrocentrism, such as Arthur Schlesinger, Jr., argue that history is a scholarly discipline, not therapy to build students' self-esteem.[5]

The perceived threat that revisionist history poses to wide sectors of the American public is clearly expressed in a *Time* magazine cover story published during the week of July 4, 1991. On the cover appears, in bold capital letters, "WHO ARE WE?" and the subtitle reads, "American kids are getting a new—and divisive—view of Thomas Jefferson, Thanksgiving and the Fourth of July." The thrust of the article is that a "growing emphasis on the nation's 'multicultural' heritage exalts racial and ethnic pride at the expense of social cohesion."

You can imagine that reading an article like this could spoil the Whitebreads' Fourth of July barbecue faster than damp charcoal. Is nothing sacred anymore—Independence Day, Thanksgiving? Will there be no national heroes left, once all their misdeeds have been exposed? While the new history is confusing and unsettling for some, others see it as a long-awaited opportunity to research and present a different set of truths.

---

[5] See Arthur Schlesinger, Jr., "History as Therapy: A Dangerous Idea," *New York Times*, 3 May 1996.

"LOOK WHAT I DISCOVERED!"

9

Understanding Institutional Racism, Sexism, and Homophobia

The question is: having described white privilege, what will I do to end it?
—Peggy McIntosh

When you think about discrimination, you probably first picture individual speech or acts occurring between two people or groups of people. This is what we might call *personal* racism, sexism, or homophobia. However, another form of discrimination that is often less understood and that may not even be acknowledged (especially by members of privileged groups) is called *institutional* discrimination.

To distinguish between the two, let's first take examples of personal bias: a group of white teens beating up a black teen after school; a teacher discouraging a female student from pursuing her plans to be an engineer; a prospective employer refusing to consider applications because they are submitted by people named David Goldberg or Ruben Gonzalez.

These examples of personal bias are blatant and overt, and those responsible can usually be readily identified. The same cannot be said for institutional discrimination, which is built into the society. You need imagination and empathy to see how the *system as a whole*—its laws and policies, its businesses, churches, government, and organizations—can put some groups at an advantage over others.

What types of disadvantages are built into the system for some people? Imagine: because you are in a wheelchair, you do not have access to many buildings and facilities. Who is responsible for the fact that you may be denied the use of schools, libraries, churches, museums, buses, and movie theaters? While it might be no one's fault in particular, this is a form of discrimination against people with disabilities and thus, in a sense, everyone's fault and everyone's responsibility. With the passage of the Americans with Disabilities Act, at least some of the institutional biases against people with disabilities are now being corrected.

In her paper *White Privilege and Male Privilege*,[1] Peggy McIntosh devises a brilliant way to demonstrate the nature and depth of institutional biases, using racism as her example. She simply makes a list of all the benefits that white people tend to have—and to take for granted—that nonwhites may not have.

---

[1] Peggy McIntosh, *White Privilege and Male Privilege: A Personal Account of Coming to See Correspondences through Work in Women's Studies.* Working Paper No. 189 (Wellesley, MA: Wellesley College Center for Research on Women, 1988).

McIntosh's own list is long, and it is devastating, but you could make an equally lengthy and disturbing list of your own. Before continuing on, try to identify at least five privileges you would put on such a list. For example, when white people wish to rent an apartment or buy a house, they can easily find neighborhoods that will welcome them.

1. _____
2. _____
3. _____
4. _____
5. _____

Now, compare your results with the following list, compiled from McIntosh's article and my own students' summaries.

In American society, whites can generally assume that

- when they go into stores, they won't automatically be eyed as potential shoplifters.
- when they go to college, they won't be thought of as "affirmative action" admits (or "affirmative action" hires in the workplace).
- when they hail a cab, the driver will stop.
- when they apply for a bank loan, they will not automatically be viewed as a bad risk.
- when they attend school or begin work, they will find role models of similar background.
- when they apply for a job, the people in power will be of their race.
- when they speak up in a group, no one will assume that they are representing anyone but themselves.
- when they turn on the television, they will

see many faces similar to theirs (there are more African Americans now than ten years ago, but still few other minorities).

- when they buy newspapers, magazines, and books, their lives and concerns will be represented.
- when they study history in school, they will learn about their own heritage.
- when they walk down the street, especially in groups or at night, they will not be perceived as a threat.

Once you begin to realize how extensive the built-in privileges are, and how much wealth, power, and influence these unearned advantages confer on the beneficiaries, you begin to understand what institutional bias is about. You start to see how lives are affected both by the big issues—housing, education, employment, health care—and by the smaller ones. If I am a person of color, are my foods and skin-care products available, especially in nonurban areas? Can I get a doll for my child that looks like him or her? Can I count on getting a pizza delivered to my home (deliveries are often not made to black—i.e., "unsafe"—neighborhoods)?

The same list-making exercise can be done to examine institutional biases against women, gays and lesbians, the elderly, the disabled, and the poor. Take some time to think about how the society discriminates against each of these groups.

If you're a member of one of them, it's usually easier to make the lists. Sometimes, however, members of the affected groups are unaware of how institutional biases work against them. They may attribute their difficulties, or failures, to their own shortcomings. They may simply accept their lesser status. Or, because they are so used to being disadvantaged, the biases may seem to be invisible. (To make such biases visible and learn to challenge them, feminists met in "consciousness-raising" groups in the 1960s and 1970s.)

Many of those who enjoy institutionalized privileges fail to see them as well. They understand that slavery and the lack of voting rights for African Americans and women are forms of institutional discrimination, but they falsely assume that since these wrongs have been corrected, our present society as a whole is fair and equal. Because they have not had to think about the many benefits they have always enjoyed, they may not know that these same benefits are denied to others, creating, in effect, second-class citizens. For example, gays and lesbians are currently struggling for what heterosexuals consider a basic right: to enter into a legally recognized marriage. Similarly, serving in the military as an openly gay or lesbian person is prohibited. Even joining the Boy Scouts of America is blocked.

A first step to dismantling institutional biases is to do our own consciousness-raising. If we're among those discriminated against, we owe it to ourselves to achieve as much clarity as possible about our own situation, perhaps in the company of others like us. If we are beneficiaries of the system, books like Judith Katz's *White Awareness*, which contains dozens of useful and thought-provoking exercises, are valuable. And we can learn a great deal about how the biases work by talking about them with friends and acquaintances— whether people of color, women, gays and lesbians, disabled, or elderly.

10

Do We Still
Need Affirmative Action?

Mend it, don't end it.
> —President Bill Clinton

Beginning with the Civil Rights Act of 1964, American society has been involved in a major social experiment to correct racial and gender discrimination of the past through a broad range of "affirmative action" laws, policies, and programs developed to provide minorities and women with more equitable access to education and employment. However, in the mid-1990s affirmative action came under vigorous attack. In 1996, for example, California became the first state to ban state-run affirmative action programs based on race, ethnicity, or sex by passing a citizen's initiative, the controversial Proposition 209. A federal judge quickly issued an injunction against the initiative on the grounds that it may be unconstitutional, and legal experts say the measure could be tied up in the courts for years before reaching the U.S. Supreme Court.

The most vocal opponents of affirmative action seem to be "angry white males" who believe they have lost jobs to less qualified women and minorities. In addition, a growing number of liberals and civil rights advocates claim that affirmative action has outlived its usefulness, as do some of its beneficiaries in the African American community (such as Supreme Court Justice Clarence Thomas; Stephen L. Carter, author of *Reflections of an Affirmative Action Baby*; and Shelby Steele, author of *The Content of Our Character*).

Affirmative action is confusing and complex, and you may find yourself among those who are uncertain as to whether to lend support or join the growing chorus of opponents. To understand what makes affirmative action so tricky, one must recall its basic premise—that those who have been behind for a long time must first be able to catch up before they can compete on an equal basis.

This underlying concept was expressed in vivid terms by President Lyndon Johnson in an oft-cited 1964 speech at Howard University:

> You do not take a person who, for years, has been hobbled by chains and liberate him, bring him to the starting line of a race and then say, "You are free to compete with all the others" and still justly believe you have been completely fair.

What this means in the workforce, for example, is that employers need to take positive, aggressive steps to ensure that women and minorities are able to take advantage of available opportunities. Such an active approach might take the form of recruiting at women's or Native American colleges, advertising job opportunities in African American magazines, or instituting programs for minority promotions.

The paradox inherent in the seemingly reasonable catch-up philosophy expressed by Johnson is, of course, that non-equal—preferential or special—treatment is necessary for a period of time to achieve equality in the future. How, ask the critics, can one advocate using color, ethnicity, and gender as criteria in employment decisions (to give one example), if one's goal is a "color-blind" society free of these criteria? How can one expect to end discrimination by practicing what the opponents label as "reverse discrimination"?

Furthermore, opponents are generally unconvinced by the argument that they are responsible for sins of the past. Why, they ask, should I have to pay for what my grandfather did to someone else's grandfather?

However you might feel about these philosophical issues, the question remains: is affirmative action working? Supporters claim that in the three main targeted areas—hiring policies, college admissions, and awarding of government contracts—significant gains have been made. For example, affirmative action is widely credited for increasing the proportion of African Americans and Latinos in white-collar occupations and helping to expand a black and Latino middle class. It has opened the door to women in exclusively male occupations, such as firefighting, police work, the military, and construction as well as in midlevel management. And it has benefited minority- and women-owned businesses that are given preferences (so-called "set-asides") in bidding for government contracts. A study by Alfred Blumrosen at Rutgers University in 1995 found that five million minority workers and six million women have better jobs because of affirmative action.

Opponents counter that these gains have come

at too great a cost. They also argue that the main beneficiaries have not been the economically or historically disadvantaged, but relatively privileged white women and well-educated members of the black, Asian, and Latino middle class as well as newly arrived immigrants who have no claim to remedies owed them for centuries of mistreatment.

The chart below summarizes the main points of contention in the affirmative action debate.

Anti-Affirmative Action	Pro-Affirmative Action
Quotas, which are inherently discriminatory, are the backbone of affirmative action.	Affirmative action relies primarily on good faith goals and timetables, not on rigid quotas; much compliance on the part of private industry is voluntary.
Abuses and fraud are rampant.	Abuses, only a small part of total affirmative action results, can be remedied.
Merit should be the only criterion for hiring, admissions, and promotions.	Our government and society routinely grant other preferences (to war veterans, senior citizens, farmers, children of university alumni, star athletes). Affirmative action candidates are no less qualified than others, and are often more qualified.
Beneficiaries of affirmative action are stigmatized and thus less effective in the workplace.	Women and people of color are often stigmatized and stereotyped regardless of affirmative action.
The resentment against affirmative action is widening the racial rift in this country.	Backlash has been exaggerated (a surprisingly large number of white men support affirmative action), and a certain degree of resentment is to be expected.

Anti-Affirmative Action	Pro-Affirmative Action
Affirmative action is really reverse discrimination.	Affirmative action is not a form of discrimination but serves only to remove its causes. Few cases of reverse discrimination have been brought by white males, and even fewer have been found justified.
White women have already caught up and no longer need assistance.	White women are far from achieving equality in the workplace. Women are still underrepresented in many professions, receive unequal pay compared to men in equivalent positions, and occupy few top positions in government and industry.
Asian Americans have made it without affirmative action, so why shouldn't others be able to do so as well?	Many Asians (especially Southeast Asian refugees) have not made it, and many others owe their success in part to affirmative action.
Help is not reaching those who need it most—the truly poor and disadvantaged, many of whom are white.	We do need additional programs to assist more people at the bottom of the socioeconomic ladder. But economic disadvantage cannot be the sole criterion, since women and minorities are discriminated against at all levels of society.

Since the summary above is necessarily brief, you might wish to take one or more of the issues separately, such as the question of abuses and fraud, and investigate further. What types of abuses are being perpetrated? How serious are they? What percentage of total affirmative action results are estimated to be fraudulent? What remedies might be possible?

Something that often remains unspoken in the debates, but that lies at the heart of affirmative action, is the whole idea of the "club." In our society, white men have been the traditional holders of power in all the "clubs"—in government, education, business and industry, and private life—and, since people tend to feel most comfortable with, and trust most, those who look, behave, and think like themselves, new "club" membership has invariably been extended to other white men. Those in power may not intend to discriminate, or even realize that they are doing so, as they cast their vote in favor of the familiar and use customary contacts (the "old boys' network") to seek out new people. That is, white men may genuinely deem other white men to be more "qualified" than women or minorities who don't fit their mental image of what a foreman, an astronaut, or a university president should be.

If affirmative action were ended now, many believe, it would be all too easy for those doing the hiring, admitting, and promoting to slip back into old patterns. Cornel West, in his best-selling book, *Race Matters*, states a clear warning: "Given the history of this country, it is a virtual certainty that without affirmative action racial and sexual discrimination would return with a vengeance."[1]

This does not mean that reform of affirmative action policies and programs is unnecessary. Even ardent supporters recognize that current policies and programs are flawed and need to be mended, perhaps completely overhauled. One necessary change is that socioeconomic class needs to be recognized along with race and gender. Those

---

[1] Cornel West, *Race Matters* (Boston: Beacon Press, 1993), 64.

whites who are battling poverty, lack of education, and joblessness need affirmative action along with (and, in some cases, more than) those currently targeted.

Also, efforts need to start much earlier in people's lives—as early as infancy and throughout the school years—to ensure that all children have an equal chance to succeed later. Current affirmative action programs address the problems much too late, usually at the time of university admission or employment. Head Start is a good example of what we might call *affirmative prevention*—the type of initiative that can help obviate the need for intervention in adulthood.

Affirmative action is hardly a policy restricted to the United States. As minority populations across the globe press for their rights, affirmative action is becoming an issue—and taking unique forms—in many countries. In Israel, for example, the universities have traditionally been opposed to affirmative action, but Tel Aviv University's law school has instituted a controversial new admissions policy, reserving a set number of places for disadvantaged students, including Jews from small towns and Israeli Arabs. In India, the decision to expand affirmative action for members of disadvantaged castes by guaranteeing places in government and the university has sparked protests and violence by members of higher castes. And in China, often misperceived by outsiders to be a homogeneous country, the Han majority has extended preferential treatment to more than fifty minority groups (not including Tibetans), allowing these groups to have more than one child and to be admitted to universities with lower examination scores.

The question on many people's minds in the United States is how long we will need some type of corrective measure, whether we call it affirmative action or something else. Opponents say the experiment has gone on for too long already; three decades is enough. They believe that we have already achieved a "level playing field." Advocates think we have barely begun to make progress and cannot expect to undo in thirty years what has been practiced for centuries. They point to the many examples of institutional racism and sexism that still pervade our society and claim that only through renewed, vigorous action can we come closer to creating the level playing field a just society demands.

11

"Give Me Your Tired...": The Immigration Myth

Day of spacious dreams!
I sailed for America,
Overblown with hope.

—Ichiyo

One of the most cherished ideas we hold about ourselves as Americans is that we welcome new-comers. Most of us, after all, are not far from the realities of immigration in our own families. If you are Latino or Asian American, you may well be a first- or second-generation immigrant. Even if you are a Whitebread and consider yourself to be 100 percent American, your family has prob-ably not been in America for more than a few gen-erations.

The enduring symbol for our nation's openness toward immigrants is the Statue of Liberty. Not only Americans but people around the world believe— or want to believe—that this is a country of hope, of refuge for all those seeking a better life. In 1783

George Washington declared America a land whose "bosom is open to receive the persecuted and oppressed of all nations."[1] The same ideal was expressed a century later by Emma Lazarus in verses carved on the pedestal of the Statue of Liberty:

> Give me your tired, your poor
> Your huddled masses
>   yearning to breathe free,
> The wretched refuse
>   of your teeming shore.
> Send these, the homeless,
>   tempest-tossed to me:
> I lift my lamp beside the golden door!

However, this poetic image of a land that welcomed immigrants seems no longer to correspond to present-day realities. Books and articles appearing in recent years use language quite different from the above to describe America's increasingly restrictive immigration policies. What was previously seen as an "open door" is now described as "half-open," "closing," "closed," or "slamming shut." We are said to be "pulling in the welcome mat," "turning away immigrants," and "narrowing the immigration gate." The memorable image is not the Statue of Liberty, but a ten-foot high, metal fence guarded by armed patrols along the U.S.-Mexico border.

The public debate over immigration in the past few years has been loud and volatile. What has emerged from the debate is hard-fought immigration legislation, passed in late 1996, which

---

[1] George Washington, "Address to the Members of the Volunteer Association and Other Inhabitants of the Kingdom of Ireland Who Have Lately Arrived in New York," in *The Writings of George Washington*, XXVII (Washington, DC: Government Printing Office, 1938), 254.

aims to tighten our borders against illegal immigrants. (While the claim is made that an estimated 300,000 people enter the country illegally each year, in truth many [recent figures suggest 41 percent] of these people actually enter the country legally and simply overstay their visas.) The new legislation includes provisions to double the size of the Border Patrol, add new fences and helicopters along the Mexican border, toughen penalties for immigrant smuggling and document fraud, and bar illegal immigrants from receiving Social Security benefits or public housing. The last provision recalls California's Proposition 187, which will deny most public benefits to illegal residents if it survives current challenges in the courts.

An exception to the current emphasis on illegal immigration is the welfare reform bill, signed into law by President Clinton in late 1996, which denies both legal and illegal immigrants access to federally funded social services, such as food stamps, Medicaid, and Supplemental Security Income (a type of cash assistance for the needy elderly, blind, and disabled). Clinton has since expressed his desire to modify this legislation as it affects legal immigrants. In response to this welfare bill, international philanthropist and naturalized U.S. citizen George Soros has donated fifty million dollars to create the Emma Lazarus Fund, which aids legal immigrants.

Especially in uncertain economic times, immigrants can easily become scapegoats, receiving blame for many of the country's woes. Fears that immigrants are taking jobs from others are widespread, and many people believe that immigrants are overusing and abusing the social welfare system. As chair of the Senate Subcommittee on Immigration, Senator Alan Simpson claimed that the American people were "fed up," adding that Americans believe "immigration has become more of a burden than a blessing."[2]

As you try to make up your own mind as to how to evaluate the economic impact of immigrants, your decision may well depend on which charts and graphs you study and which reports you read. Anti-immigrant reports often argue that unskilled or low-skilled laborers, including many African Americans and "old" minorities, are severely hurt by the loss of jobs to "new" minorities. The cost of providing services to immigrants and their children is shown to be an enormous drain on the economy as a whole as well as on individual taxpayers, threatening, for example, the entire state of California with "economic and social bankruptcy," according to the ballot initiative for Proposition 187.

An entirely different picture of the economic impact emerges from research undertaken by immigration specialists at the Urban Institute and elsewhere. Facts and figures compiled by the Urban Institute demonstrate that immigrants are less likely to be on welfare than U.S.-born residents and that they pay much more in taxes than they receive in public services. As dramatic confirmation of the immigrants' contribution to the economy, a 1995 study financed by the Rand Corporation shows that the state, federal, and local taxes immigrants pay each year exceed the services they receive by $25 to $30 billion.

------

[2] Linda Ocasio, "The Year of the Immigrant as Scapegoat," in *NACLA: Report on the Americas* 29, no. 3 (November/December 1995): 15.

Moreover, pro-immigration analysts argue that immigrants take few jobs from others, since undocumented workers often do hard, tedious labor at low wages. They perform difficult jobs no one wants to accept, as fruit pickers and maids, for example; and entire industries, such as agriculture and garment manufacturing, depend on this immigrant labor. As for the legal immigrants, a significant number are granted their status only after documenting that no Americans possess the necessary qualifications for the highly specialized positions they occupy in medicine, information technology, and academic research.

The pro-immigrationists further bolster their claim that immigrants are good for the economy by citing the many jobs and billions of dollars generated by immigrant entrepreneurs. Far beyond the stereotypes of Chinese restaurants and Korean grocery stores, immigrants are founding new businesses—among them a number of the country's most successful high-tech companies—and attracting foreign investment.

In an insightful article, "The New Economics of Immigration," George J. Borjas argues that immigration results in both economic gains and losses for the native population. As he explains, the "winners and losers are typically different groups," and "policy parameters can be set in ways that attempt to maximize gains and minimize losses."[3]

Aside from the economic arguments, uneasiness over demographics is also fueling anti-immigration sentiment. The changing complexion of America, the so-called "browning" of the country referred to in chapter 1, causes some people

---

[3] George J. Borjas, "The New Economics of Immigration," *Atlantic Monthly*, November 1996, 80.

to favor drastic cutbacks in immigration and prompts others to call for a moratorium. The question about whom to let in and whom to exclude goes to the heart of what it means to be an American.

Of course, the immigration question is not new. Throughout our history, it has been posed again and again and answered in different ways. A quick survey of immigration attitudes and policies shows that the young nation did indeed welcome most newcomers during the initial periods of growth and expansion, but there were notable exceptions. Attempts were made, for example, during the colonial era to exclude "undesirables" such as Roman Catholics, Quakers, and convicts. Later, so-called Nativists were influential in keeping out "foreign elements" such as Irish Catholics. Near the end of the nineteenth century, entry restrictions were first enacted into law, and in 1891 the Immigration and Naturalization Service (INS) was created to regulate and enforce immigration laws, which have since evolved into a highly complex body of legislation.

Those who criticize immigration policy over the past century point to the shameful and abundant evidence of discrimination against those whose nationality, religion, or political views did not match the prevailing profile of a desirable immigrant. A few examples suffice to show that the reputed open door has been more myth than reality for some time. The Chinese Exclusion Act of 1882 (not repealed until 1943), prohibited Chinese laborers from entering the country and denied the possibility of citizenship to those already here. The Immigration Act of 1924 (not repealed until 1965) established a system of quotas by national origin that effectively stopped the massive influx of southern and eastern Europeans, whose darker complexions made them less welcome than those from northern and western Europe. And the Immigration and Nationality Act of 1952 (the McCarran-Walter Act) allowed for the exclusion of those whose political views were believed to threaten the democratic process.

Should you investigate our immigration history, you will also find disturbing evidence of less than humanitarian responses to refugee crises around the world. Historians have documented the U.S. failure to harbor victims of the Holocaust in the 1930s, a failure that included refusals to grant special visas to Jewish refugee children. More recent examples include the hard stance taken by the Bush and Reagan administrations against Haitian and Salvadoran asylum seekers and a longstanding reluctance to admit political refugees from African countries.

On the other hand, there have been significant successes and achievements on the part of both the government and individual citizens. Since 1965, immigration law has been liberalized to reflect greater ethnic, racial, and religious tolerance. In fact, the backlash we are now experiencing is due in large part to this more equitable approach. And although some refugee groups have been turned away, thousands of others, notably Cubans, Indochinese, and Soviet Jews, have been provided haven. Many Americans have worked tirelessly to rescue friends and relatives from overseas refugee camps, and churches and volunteer agencies have helped hundreds of thousands of newcomers adapt.

In the public mind, highly publicized incidents and crises evoke a complex response of sympathy, resentment, and fear. The 1980 Mariel boat lift, intended as a humanitarian response by Jimmy Carter, resulted in untold problems as Castro deported criminals and mental patients. The fates of other "boat people" and refugees (Vietnamese, Haitian, Cuban, and Chinese) have repeatedly captured media attention. After languishing for up to twenty years in resettlement camps in Indochina, the last of tens of thousands of Vietnamese are being repatriated, many by force, to Vietnam. The 1993 grounding of the *Golden Venture*, carrying almost three hundred Chinese passengers to be smuggled into New York, dramatized the peril and suffering undergone by hopeful present-day immigrants.

As the numbers of refugees globally have continued to climb to the present staggering figure of twenty-three million, the moral dilemma has intensified. In a world in which the United States still represents opportunity and safety to millions of people, the challenge is to find new ways to respond that are at once humane and realistic.

12

Do Americans Speak English Only or English Plus?

The great challenge, beauty, and promise of our age is the way in which it allows us to become fluent in the languages of a hundred cultures.

—Pico Iyer

It would no doubt come as a surprise to many Americans to learn that English is not the legally established language of the land. Though English does function as our common language—in government, business, courts, schools, and most other institutions—the U.S. Constitution remains silent on the subject, and no subsequent federal legislation establishes a national language.

The silence of the Constitution on this matter is seen by some as the wisdom of our forefathers and by others as a major oversight. In recent years a furious debate has been raging on the question of whether to officialize English. Few multicultural issues cause people to feel such high emotion—whether fear, passion, or loyalty—as does language. At one end of the spectrum, groups like the one known as U.S. English are working to restrict the use of languages other than English; at the other end are those who have founded English Plus, an organization favoring bilingualism or multilingualism for all Americans.

The English-only advocates tend to see English both as an essential tool for survival and as a stamp of Americanism. They are offended by some immigrants' failure to learn the language, interpreting this as a lack of respect for or gratitude to their adopted country. They resent hearing conversations they do not understand in supermarkets, in the workplace, or on the airwaves. They are also concerned that there will be no glue to hold the country together without a mandated common language.

An anecdote which illustrates the attitude of these Americans is told by Carlos Alberto Montaner, a native of Cuba who writes occasional pieces for Miami's *El Nuevo Herald*:

> I was walking quietly with my wife on a sidewalk in Miami Beach. We were speaking Spanish, of course, because that is our language. Suddenly, we were accosted by a spry little old lady, wearing a baseball cap and sneakers, who told us: "Talk English. You are in the United States." She continued on her way at once, without stopping to see our reaction. The expression on her face, curiously, was not that of somebody performing a rude action, but of somebody performing a sacred patriotic duty.[1]

---

[1] Carlos Alberto Montaner, "Talk English—You Are in the United States," in *Language Loyalties: A Source Book on the Official English Controversy*, edited by James Crawford (Chicago: University of Chicago Press, 1992), 163.

What is happening with the English language across the country is much more than simply a question of the outrage of little old ladies. The drive to make English official is being led by several powerful, well-financed lobbying organizations, including the above-mentioned U.S. English and English First. These groups are working to pass English language amendments (ELAs) on the state level, with the eventual goal of adding such an ELA to the U.S. Constitution. To date, more than twenty states have passed official-English legislation, though thus far these statutes tend to be largely ceremonial. The 1988 Arizona ELA, struck down by lower courts, went before the Supreme Court in 1996. The U.S. Congress is also involved in the English-only debate; in 1996 the House of Representatives, but not the Senate, passed a bill requiring that English be the official language of the federal government.

Numerous scholars and critics believe that the real motivation of ELA organizers is racism, targeted primarily at Latinos and Asians. Harvey Daniels, editor of *Not Only English*, describes the movement as "another cycle of bigotry disguised as a debate about language."[2] Similarly, James Crawford, author of *Hold Your Tongue*, writes about the phenomenon he calls "Hispanophobia" that is fueling the ELA movement.[3]

While these charges of racism may in fact hold true for some English-only leaders and propo-

---

[2] Harvey A. Daniels, ed., *Not Only English: Affirming America's Multicultural Heritage* (Urbana, IL: National Council of Teachers of English, 1990), ix.

[3] James Crawford, *Hold Your Tongue: Bilingualism and the Politics of "English Only"* (Reading, MA: Addison-Wesley, 1992), chapter 6.

nents, prejudice alone cannot explain the support nationwide for officializing English. As with so many multicultural issues, well-intentioned, concerned people find themselves facing yet another dilemma. After all, what's wrong with the idea that immigrants ought to learn the language? Is it not to their advantage to learn English as quickly as possible? How can the nation function if there is no common means of communication? Why should state and federal funds be used to assist those who don't understand English by providing services such as bilingual ballots and bilingual education? Haven't immigrants managed perfectly well in the past without all of these extra services?

Such questions are critical to an understanding of the debate. In response, English-Plus adherents readily agree that immigrants must learn English. But they point out that English language acquisition is continuing in much the same way as has always been the pattern (except for isolationist groups such as the Amish). That is, the first generation often remains tied to the native tongue, with English being used little or imperfectly. (If you have attempted to learn a foreign language yourself, you will understand how difficult it is to achieve a reasonable level of fluency and how natural it is, no matter where you go in the world, to prefer your mother tongue.) Studies show that second-generation children often know both languages, but English already tends to dominate. By the third generation, the children know only English and usually have no real ability to function in their grandparents' language. Thus, contrary to what English-only adherents fear, research indicates that it's the immigrants' language that is endangered, not English!

Immigrants themselves are the first to recognize the importance of learning English. In many cities and towns, they are on long waiting lists for scarce places in adult language classes and often study in the evening, after a full day of work. A survey administered in Dade County, Florida, revealed that 98 percent of Hispanic parents wanted their children to become "perfectly" fluent in English.[4]

What about the familiar glue question? Those who believe in English Plus say this is a nonissue, since Americans do in fact have a common language. They argue that such a large percentage of the population already knows English and the incentives for the others to learn it are so powerful, we need hardly be concerned. Not only is English unthreatened as our national language, but it is the undisputed international language, used all over the world in business, science, computers and technology, airports and air-traffic control, tourism, conferences, diplomacy, medicine, sports, advertising, and pop music. Why cause needless problems in an attempt to achieve by coercion what is already a fact of life?

Let's take a look at some of these potential problems. The most obvious is the clash with First Amendment rights. How, critics of ELA ask, can a nation that believes so fervently in individual freedom and holds freedom of speech so sacred prohibit citizens from using their own language, or, for that matter, any language of choice? To many, it seems absurd even to contemplate such a violation of the values that Americans cherish.

Freedom of speech is not the only right that could be jeopardized. Without bilingual ballots,

---

[4] Ibid., 97.

translation services in courts, and similar assistance, other rights guaranteed by the U.S. Constitution or by federal statutes, such as the right to vote and the right to due process of the law, would also be threatened.

Furthermore, how far would the prohibitions go on using languages other than English, and how could they possibly be enforced? Horror stories already abound of individuals being fired or discriminated against because of language. A shocking example that prompted much national attention was that of a mother involved in a routine custody case in San Antonio, Texas, in the summer of 1995. Severely reprimanded by the judge for speaking Spanish at home with her five-year-old daughter, the mother was told she was "abusing" the child and could lose custody if she did not speak English with her in the home.[5]

Now to the question of taxpayers' money. Angered at what they view as excessive public expenditures, U.S. English members have targeted a wide variety of bilingual services for elimination in one or more states. If members of this group have their way, languages other than English could be prohibited on signs, driver's license regulations and tests, radio and television broadcasts, transportation schedules, and voting materials as well as in public schools and hospitals.

Those who favor multilingual policies and English Plus respond that these services are essential to protect immigrants' health, safety, and basic rights. They recognize the costs involved but oppose moving backward to a system characterized by a "sink or swim" philosophy. They explain

---

[5] Sam Howe Verhovek, "Mother Scolded by Judge for Speaking in Spanish," *New York Times*, 30 August 1995.

that while it may seem that the immigrants of previous generations did perfectly well without assistance, it's much more likely that many did poorly: never venturing far from home, not being able to defend themselves in court, dropping out of school, and not even being able to obtain emergency assistance or understand what treatment they were getting in a hospital.

Of the various services and programs currently provided, one that arouses consistent controversy is bilingual education. A product of the civil rights movement, bilingual education finds its philosophical underpinning in Title VI of the Civil Rights Act of 1964, which prohibits denial of equal educational opportunity on the basis of race, language, or national origin. With the passage of the Bilingual Education Act in 1968, programs received federal funding and began to grow significantly. Though this legislation authorized funding for instructional materials, teacher training, and research, it surprisingly did not specifically require that languages other than English be used in the classroom. The 1974 Supreme Court decision in *Lau v. Nichols* obligated schools to assist students of limited English proficiency, and bilingual education, though not mandated, was suggested as one of several options to provide the required help.

The theory behind bilingual education is, quite simply, that students should receive instruction in their native language while they are learning English. Today most educators, and even the most ardent critics of bilingual education, recognize that some transition period between predominant use of the native language and use of English is necessary and that the "all or nothing" approach is too brutal—and too unsuccessful.

To understand bilingual education, one needs to know that it encompasses a wide variety of philosophies, pedagogical methods, and approaches. Some supporters of bilingual education advocate learning English as quickly as possible in order to mainstream students, while others believe in a slower acquisition over several years, all the while ensuring that students maintain skills in their native language. In recent years, innovative two-way bilingual programs have been developed that allow students who speak only English to learn a second language (e.g., Spanish) in the same classroom with those (Spanish speakers) who are learning English.

To give an example of one model, beginning English students take a combination of courses in their first year: most of these are in their native language (language arts, math, science, and social studies); one or more are in so-called "sheltered English," where students learn English with other non-native speakers; and several are in "mainstream English" (art, music, and physical education) alongside native speakers. Over a period of years, the emphasis shifts, until the students are completely mainstreamed, except for one enrichment course in their native language.

Whatever the particular philosophy or methodology (and there is obviously room for many different ideas and approaches), the hard fact remains that bilingual programs need funding. In fact, the failure of many programs thus far seems to derive less from flaws in the concept of bilingual education than from a lack of funding to ensure that personnel, materials, and research are sufficient to the task. But how can one justify the significant amounts of money that must be spent to support the programs? The answer can only be found in a realistic assessment of the benefits to society of bilingual education (and bilingualism) and of the costs to society of ignoring the needs these programs fill.

Among those who defend bilingual education and oppose English-only movements are Teachers of English to Speakers of Other Languages (TESOL) and the National Council of Teachers of English (NCTE). Members of these organizations agree with the philosophy of English Plus that in our multicultural, multilingual, increasingly interdependent world, there is no more enlightened policy than to promote bilingualism for all Americans. According to English Plus, the knowledge of other languages in addition to English "contributes to our nation's productivity, worldwide competitiveness, and successful international diplomacy."[6]

As laudable as this philosophy sounds, practical matters will need to be addressed and resolved. Should physicians and nurses from other countries, for example, be allowed to practice medicine if they have not mastered English? Should those who cannot read English street signs be eligible for a driver's license? What about university teaching assistants who may command excellent reading and writing skills but are not understood by their students? These and numerous other thorny issues will not be remedied by a quick fix, but will require careful study and ongoing commitments.

---

[6] "The English Plus Alternative," in *Language Loyalties*, edited by James Crawford (Chicago: University of Chicago Press, 1992), 152.

13

What Is PC? Are You PC?

All right, I'll admit it: I'm afraid I'm not politically correct, while, at the same time, I'm afraid I don't want to be politically correct, while simultaneously being afraid I don't know what the hell being politically correct is.

—Averie La Russa,
Former Student,
University of Pennsylvania

The student quoted above is not alone in her confusion and fear. What does it mean to be politically correct (PC)? Why are people so afraid of being associated with it? What exactly is the huge fuss over political correctness all about?

For over a decade we've been bombarded by books, articles, and media reports on the PC debates. There are so many false accusations and misunderstandings on both sides that it's hard to sort out what the real issues are and figure out with whom to agree.

To understand PC, you might imagine that you have two friends: Rosa, a Chicana, and Lars, a

Swedish American. Rosa is proud of her Mexican heritage and disturbed when she encounters negative stereotypes and general disregard for her culture. She tries to remind others to be more sensitive, asking them, for example, to use the term *Chicana* (denoting a Mexican American female) rather than *Hispanic* or *Latina*, words she finds too general. At her university, she belongs to an activist group that is pushing for more Chicano and Chicana faculty as well as curricular changes, including the long-range goal of implementing a Chicano Studies program. She also wants more Mexican Americans to assume leadership positions in government and business, and she is glad that holidays such as Cinco de Mayo are being more widely celebrated.

Lars says that he is not prejudiced against Chicanos, but he thinks Rosa is demanding too much too fast. He does not, for example, think that the university should spend money on Chicano Studies to appease a relatively small group of students. Offended that Rosa insists on so many changes, he accuses her of being "politically correct"—of going overboard in championing her rights and of making excessive, unrealistic demands. He resents the fact that she is imposing her own agenda and her own notion of what constitutes acceptable speech and behavior on everyone else.

Not unexpectedly, Rosa rejects the PC label, seeing herself as combating intolerance and fighting for her rights in the best tradition of American democracy. She finds Lars's label insulting, since it suggests that she herself is narrow-minded, intolerant, and, worst of all, undemocratic. Lars has told her that she seems unwilling to compromise or allow for different viewpoints;

she always gives him the impression that her way is the only right way. She responds that she should not be expected to compromise on issues of basic human rights.

As this example illustrates, the label "politically correct" that Lars uses further polarizes the debate. At first, opponents of multiculturalism used the label *PC* to describe perceived excessive or outlandish demands, such as insisting that *woman* be spelled "womyn." The label caught on so quickly, however, and proved to be such a potent weapon, that now any effort associated with diversity or multiculturalism can quickly be discredited by crying "PC!" The strategy seems a brilliant one, since it's hard to find anyone these days who wants to be seen as politically correct. (In return, multiculturalists can ward off any challenges or criticism by crying "Racist!" or "Sexist!"—infuriating their critics and stifling further dialogue; see chapter 6.)

In the media coverage of the PC debate, headlines have warned of PC "tyranny" and "totalitarianism." Magazines like *Newsweek* and *Time* have been producing negative reports for some time now, decrying the dangers of PC thinking. For example, a *Newsweek* cover story entitled "Thought Police" asked the question: "Is this the new enlightenment on campus or the new McCarthyism?"[1] Syndicated columnist Mona Charen wrote as early as 1990 of the "modern Inquisition" on college campuses,[2] and *New York Times* reporter Richard Bernstein gave his book on multiculturalism the title, *Dictatorship of Virtue.*

---

[1] *Newsweek*, 24 December 1990, 48-55.
[2] Mona Charen, "Thought Police Control Campus," *Oregonian*, 9 December 1990.

In addition to accusing multiculturalists of being dictators, critics also charge them with being separatists and tribalists who have forgotten the common goals of the country. By recognizing (and thus emphasizing) difference, the argument goes, multiculturalists are dividing our society, tearing apart its very fabric. This is what Arthur Schlesinger, Jr., calls the "disuniting" of America and Robert Hughes calls the "fraying" of America. Attacks of this nature recall the issues discussed in chapter 2 and are in fact a different formulation of the old melting pot debate.

The most effective weapon in the anti-PC arsenal has been humor. At every opportunity, multiculturalists are made to look ridiculous. One of the most ingenious attacks has come from Brown University graduate Jeff Shesol, whose comic strip, "Thatch," first published in his campus paper, rapidly received nationwide attention.[3] Dressed like Superman, Shesol's main cartoon character, Politically Correct Person, attempts in an earnest way to fight insensitive behavior wherever it lurks. However, he almost always just ends up looking foolish. Another example of the anti-PC humor industry is the popular series of politically correct bedtime stories.

How have the multiculturalists responded to this ongoing mockery? While some effective responses have emerged, the counterattack has not been as clever or as forceful as the attack. Books by Gerald Graff, Henry Louis Gates, Jr., Stanley Fish, and John K. Wilson do illuminate the issues and present the other side, but their works have not reached a wide audience or affected the general consciousness in the way that writings by

---

[3] Jeff Shesol, *Thatch* (New York: Random House, 1991).

Arthur Schlesinger, Jr., Richard Bernstein, Dinesh D'Souza, William Bennett, Allan Bloom, George Will, and E. D. Hirsch, Jr., have.

In the multiculturalists' defense, we can remind ourselves that bringing about change is much more difficult than resisting change. The critics have the weight of tradition on their side, and they occupy many of the key positions in the mainstream media. Furthermore, well-funded conservative foundations and think tanks have for some time been engaged in efforts to attack political correctness, lending support to research, lawsuits, and campus newspapers. Clearly, the preponderance of money on the side of tradition- alists helps to explain why the multiculturalists have fared so poorly.

So, do you consider yourself to be PC? A lot may depend on definitions. If being PC means acting in sanctimonious ways, losing one's sense of humor, and forcing opinions on others, then you most likely will wish to distance yourself. But if it means standing up against degrading, abu- sive words and actions, then you are probably in sympathy with PC thinking.

In his thoughtful essay, "How I'm PC," Joel Conarroe describes the dilemma: "To protest de- meaning language or ideas is to run the risk of being labeled 'PC,'...but not to protest is often to tolerate the intolerable." Conarroe gives several examples of documented campus behavior, such as holding "slave auctions" at fraternity houses and wearing T-shirts that say, "Club Faggots, Not Seals." He concludes his essay with this question: "Does feeling compelled to speak out against these and other examples of intolerance make me politically correct? If so, count me in."[4]

When considering your own position, you might also reexamine the commonly expressed argument that multiculturalists are operating from a political agenda, whereas the defenders of the system are not. As Gerald Graff points out, the "rule seems to be that any politics is suspect except the kind that helped us get where we are, which by definition does not count as politics."[5] Graff explains that, contrary to popular belief, wishing to maintain the status quo is just as political as wishing to change it. Accordingly, he claims that the PC advocates should not be seen as trying to impose their views any more than their opponents are. It's just that the views of the opponents happen to be in place already.

Rather than getting hung up on the term *PC*, we might exercise the option just to end this particular debate and move ahead. The multiculturalists have been outmaneuvered; they have probably lost the PC battle, at least in the public's mind. But that doesn't mean they should not be devising new strategies and, above all, getting on with their work. What is at stake, and what has been lost all too often in the PC debate, is still the fundamental challenge of creating a society that is more inclusive of all the people—in short, a more democratic society that renounces the denigration of its members.

Thus, whatever our politics, the task may well be to get "beyond PC" (this is the title of an excellent book edited by Pat Aufderheide). In that spirit, the next chapters of this book are dedicated to concrete strategies for change.

---

[4] Joel Conarroe, "How I'm PC," *New York Times*, 12 July 1991.
[5] Graff, *Beyond the Culture Wars*, 156.

14

On Becoming Multicultural: Rolling Up Your Sleeves

We have a world to conquer, one person at a time, starting with ourselves.
—Nikki Giovanni

As a person interested in multiculturalism, at a certain point you'll want to get practical, break out of some old patterns, and make concrete changes in your life. The next few chapters are designed to help point you in new directions. Here are several initial suggestions to get you under way, so that you can understand yourself better in multicultural terms and prepare for more meaningful multicultural encounters.

1. Explore Your Own Cultural Identity

A key to functioning successfully in a multicultural environment is knowing more about your own cultural identity. The good news is that you are already multicultural. No matter what your background, you most certainly belong to or identify with a variety of different groups or subgroups. Some are more important to you than others, some may change over your lifetime, and some may be chosen and others not.

Take time to think about this and do some investigating. How would you describe who you are and where you fit in? Have you ever examined your own "roots"? Do you find yourself relating to certain parts of your family tree more than others? To what extent do you identify yourself as an American? Do you have strong ties to a particular geographical region? What about your religious ties? Professional or other affiliations? Do you speak "standard" English? Other languages? Can you begin to see how certain values you hold derive from your cultural background(s)?

Understanding your own cultural makeup helps you to be more receptive to the variety in other people's backgrounds. If you are white, don't make the mistake of thinking that this is "all" you are and that you "have no culture." Because yours is the predominant culture, it may just seem as if you have nothing to distinguish yourself from others. Learn more about your particular brand of "whiteness" as well as about your other cultural identities growing out of your religion, profession, geographical location, and so on. The more you understand about these multiple identities, the more you will realize how cultural stereotyping distorts by oversimplifying (see chapter 4).

2. Develop an "Outsider" Mentality

As you review your personal cultural inventory, some parts of your identity will likely be more mainstream than others. Concentrate for a moment on the parts that are more characteristic of the outsider. You may, for example, be a white, heterosexual, able-bodied male, but perhaps you hate sports. Or you are a nurse. Or maybe you are very short. Consider what it is about you or your experience that puts you in a minority position. Or simply recall a time when you were definitely not a member of the ingroup.

Now, focus on this experience of "otherness," of not belonging, of being an outsider. How would you describe the emotions involved? How do you cope with being an outsider?

The "outsider" mentality needs to be available to you all the time. It will help you to understand other outsiders. They need not be Mormon, or male nurses, but they will likely be undergoing many of the same feelings and frustrations associated with being excluded, being powerless, being looked down upon. Whenever you're having trouble understanding the dynamics of a cross-cultural conflict, recall your own "outsider-ness" to help you empathize with, and take seriously, feelings you might otherwise dismiss. It will also give you insight into strategies for including others who may feel marginalized.

3. Relax, Relax, Relax

Try not to be uptight in cross-cultural encounters. A little nervousness is to be expected; the other person is probably nervous, too, about meeting or interacting with you.

Realize that you convey a message not only with your actual words, but also with your body language. Try to loosen up. When you're tense, you give off negative signals by your posture, facial expressions, eye contact, and the tone of your voice. Think consciously about slowing down, and take a deep breath.

Part of relaxing is not fearing mistakes. As you interact with new people, you're bound to do and say the wrong thing at times. While some of your mistakes will be embarrassing, some hurtful, and some silly, none is likely to be fatal, and most can be repaired. If, for example, you tell a Chinese American acquaintance how much you like sushi, you might just apologize and remember to be more careful next time. When you err, don't be too hard on yourself, and be gracious with others when they err.

As you encounter people who are very different from you, you'll probably be unsure just how much to focus on the differences between you. Should you ignore them altogether and act as if you are just two ordinary people? Should you talk about them openly? Again, relaxing and acting natural is a key, but this doesn't mean pretending that differences don't exist. A good tip comes from the African American poet Pat Parker in her poem, "For the white person who wants to know how to be my friend." Parker writes: "The first thing you do is to forget that i'm black. Second, you must never forget that i'm black."[1]

Keep your sense of humor always. A sense of humor is undoubtedly the single most important ingredient in cross-cultural interactions. Feel free to laugh at yourself and with others. Laughter creates bonds and heals wounds. It helps us relax. It reminds us that we are all rather frail human creatures with more in common than we may have realized.

4. Suspend Judgment

As you venture out into new multicultural territory, you'll hear ideas and encounter ways of be-

---

[1] Pat Parker, *Movement in Black: The Collected Poetry of Pat Parker 1961-1978* (Ithaca, NY: Firebrand Books, 1978), 68.

having that are completely new to you, some of which will seem strange, some objectionable or offensive. The best multicultural advice possible is to put off value judgments while you try to absorb, reflect on, and relate to what the other person is saying. Peter Elbow, author of *Embracing Contraries*, calls this the "Believing Game," in which you allow yourself temporarily to believe that the other person is telling the truth before jumping in with critiques, objections, and disagreements.[2] Elbow asks us to put aside critical thinking until we have had a chance to see the other person's side. Clearly, this technique of suspending disbelief requires careful listening.

If, for example, a Cherokee Indian student living in your dormitory mentions to you that he is offended by the name of your football team ("The Big U Cherokees"), don't tell him he's being oversensitive, or point out that the team has had that name for fifty years, or claim he should be flattered by the attention. Try first to look at the situation from his point of view and to find out from him why he's upset, or in other words, try to empathize with him.

5. Be Willing to Teach Others about Yourself

What if you commonly find yourself in settings where you're in the minority and people know little about you? While you may be perfectly willing to explain yourself to others once or twice, what happens when this becomes a steady obligation?

As any American who has traveled abroad knows, becoming a spokesperson for an entire group can be difficult and taxing. Americans

---

[2] Peter Elbow, *Embracing Contraries: Explorations in Learning and Teaching* (New York: Oxford University Press), chapter 12.

abroad may be asked to explain and justify U.S. foreign policy, to sing American folk songs, or to expound on everything from the stock market to the NBA.

Back home, if you're an ethnic minority—or, for example, a Jew in a Christian neighborhood, a woman in an all-male corporation, a wheelchair user in a university—you're probably well aware of the demands placed on you. Not only must you perform ably (since you are so visible, your mistakes are also quite visible), but you have the double burden of functioning as teacher. The teacher role may be unwanted, but it is thrust upon you.

While it may be a burden to be called upon to teach and explain, it's also a privilege. Some will find themselves in this role much more frequently than others, but we are all in it at some time, and we need to muster as much patience, and love, as possible to help those around us understand who we are. Although you may at first have few answers and feel inadequate to the task, with practice you can eventually become quite skilled.

6. Let Curiosity Override Fear

If a sense of humor is the most critical element in cross-cultural success, curiosity is certainly close behind. Maybe you're shy or insecure, maybe you're afraid of being rejected or of looking like a fool. While inhibitions will keep you within familiar bounds, a healthy sense of curiosity will draw you out. Let your natural interest in other people, your sense of wonder about why they behave as they do, override your anxieties. Think about how much more you'll know about the world and the people in it if you are able to give free reign to your curiosity.

15

Asking Questions That Take You "Inside"

Multicultural education is not about dividing a united nation, but about uniting a deeply divided nation.
—James Banks

If you're dealing with an entirely new culture, you'll begin on the outside, and the sense of unfamiliarity can be intense. You may feel almost as if you're in a foreign country, looking in on foods, dress, music, arts, language, and—above all—values that are not your own. You may experience a form of "culture shock," a sense of confusion and alienation similar to what travelers abroad undergo. The culture shock, for example, experienced by a group of American hearing students visiting a local school for the deaf can be as powerful as that of American students visiting Japan.

One of the best ways to overcome the estrangement of encountering a new culture is to ask questions. What do you most want to find out about cultural groups other than your own? What are you most interested in learning? You'll find that your multicultural education will mean more to you, if you learn how to ask your own questions. Asking questions is usually a matter of following your nose, of starting with what you want to know and pursuing your own interests. Above all, don't be afraid to begin with what might seem to be too-elementary questions. (Why do Muslims fast? What exactly is Ramadan? How does American Sign Language work?) Inevitably, one question, even the most basic one, leads to another, and you'll find yourself looking at issues that are challenging, interconnected, and profound. Whatever your particular questions might be, you can look for answers in books, the arts, and the media (see chapter 16), by traveling (see chapter 17), or by talking with people.

You can start, for example, with curiosity about names you've come across in the arts or the media. Perhaps you've heard about Cornel West but haven't yet read *Race Matters*. Or you've noticed Spike Lee's videos on the shelf but haven't seen *Do the Right Thing* or *Malcolm X*. Or maybe you've heard about the African American festival Kwanzaa and would like to know more. Looking into what the ceremonies, symbols, and foods of Kwanzaa represent can quickly immerse you in aspects of African American history and reveal much about contemporary values and concerns in the black community.

In all your explorations, you'll want to gain insights into the "insider's perspective." This doesn't mean that you become an insider or necessarily adopt that perspective, but rather that you begin to see how and why someone might think differently from you. Moving closer to the insider's perspective means that you begin to "get it." If you're an American learning about France, for example, it doesn't mean that you become French, but you can begin to see the world "through French eyes."

As you begin to get inside, you'll see that certain markers of identity—names, places, and events—mean little or nothing to you but carry significant emotional weight within the group. And you'll discover that the meaning you attach to certain things may be very different from that expressed by group members. When learning more about African Americans, for example, you'll find that identity-shaping concepts and experiences might include

Marcus Garvey
Underground Railroad
Letter from a Birmingham Jail
Dred Scott decision
Amistad mutiny
Howard Beach incident
Black Panthers
Harlem Renaissance
Jim Crow segregation
Watts riots
Brotherhood of Sleeping Car Porters
East St. Louis riots (1917)
"Red Summer" of 1919
Plessy v. Ferguson
Montgomery bus boycott
One Million Man March on Washington
Niagara Movement (1905)
Brown v. Board of Education

Similarly, one can learn a great deal by asking what Wounded Knee, the Black Hills, and Sitting Bull mean to the Lakota Sioux. Or the Stonewall riots and Harvey Milk to gays and lesbians. Or Angel Island and Manzanar to Japanese Americans.

While this type of questioning can give you a sense of a cultural group's historical identity and consciousness, another set of questions leads more into sociopolitical identity. For example, what questions might you ask to find out more about how Latinos define their own lives and problems? What are the main concerns of Latinos in your area? How would you find this out?

Again, begin with an area of interest to you personally. If you're a university student, you can look at your own campus. How large is the Latino student population? How are Latinos affected by recruitment policies, scholarships, housing? Are there Latino professors? Administrators? How does the curriculum reflect Latino history and culture? How would you describe the social patterns on campus regarding friendships and dating between Latinos and others?

Or if you are working with Latinos in your company or organization, you might wish to learn more about how they feel about their working conditions. Are they satisfied with their opportunities for employment and promotion? Are they treated with respect by coworkers and management? Do they feel they have special talents or skills that are being sufficiently utilized? Do they have special needs or requests, and, if so, how has the company responded?

An unexpected benefit of your multicultural investigation is that you'll inevitably learn more about yourself and your own culture(s). After all, as you look at another group, you're always comparing and contrasting it with your own. You'll realize that you may not be as familiar with your own culture as you had thought, or as you wish to be, and that you can approach it in much the same way as you do others, asking many of the same questions. If you are Christian, for example, in thinking about Ramadan you might begin to understand better what distinguishes your own observances.

A final note: of course, there is no one insider's perspective on any culture. To assume this would be to fall into the error of stereotyping. Nonetheless, the concept is useful as a way of suggesting that when we learn about other cultures, we are not just becoming familiar with facts and figures, but also with different ways of interpreting, relating to, and making sense of the world.

16

Discovering the Alternative Media

*We've realized that the most challenging
and interesting voices of our time are still
not published with any great frequency
by the mainstream media.*
                                   —Eric Utne

As you explore U.S. cultures, you'll find that the
most popular, accessible, and familiar media
sources are severely limited in their presentation
of minorities. What we are exposed to every day
on television and radio, in the press, and at the
movies is still largely presented from a mainstream, Whitebread point of view. Whether you
tune to ABC, CBS, NBC, or CNN, you get the same
news. And whether you read *Time, Newsweek,* or
U.S. News and World Report, you get the same
types of stories, presented in much the same familiar way.

Why do the mainstream media provide such
partial and inadequate coverage of our multicultural society? First, and obviously, the media are
owned and controlled by the powerful and

117

wealthy, whose interests are generally not in sympathy with those on the outside. And, historically, very few people of color and other minorities have been represented on the staffs of major television stations, newspapers, or magazines, making it unlikely that the concerns of their communities would receive fair or adequate coverage.

To hear the many voices of our multicultural society—particularly those voices largely missing from the mainstream media—you'll want to explore the alternative press. Here a rich, fascinating world of ideas flourishes, and criticism of the status quo is loud and clear. There are hundreds of alternative newspapers and magazines available, and the moment you begin to read, you'll see how mainstream the mainstream is. In the alternative press, everything from the feature stories to the advertising, from the cartoons and editorials to the want ads is different.

If you're interested in women's issues, you might begin with *Ms.* or *On the Issues.* If you would like to know more about what matters to African Americans, pick up *Emerge, Essence, Ebony,* or *Jet.* The primary magazines for gays and lesbians are *The Advocate, Out,* and *Poz.* Native American newspapers and periodicals include *Indian Country Today, Whispering Wind, American Indian Quarterly,* and *Native Peoples.* Remember, you don't have to be a person with disabilities to read *The Disability Rag, Ability,* or *Deaf Issues,* and you don't have to be Latino to subscribe to *Hispanic* or *Hispanic News.* These publications offer a window into worlds that you might otherwise not even see.

If you want to get your feet wet but don't know quite what interests you, pick up a copy of the *Utne Reader* at a magazine stand. Every other month, Eric Utne and his staff put together a compilation of articles from the alternative media, ranging from "Buddhism American Style" to "Class Bias on Campus." You'll find lots of information here on alternative sources, with addresses. Similarly, the magazine *Alternative Press Review*, which calls itself "your guide beyond the mainstream," can help you find available periodicals, books, and films. And when you're in a large bookstore, browse through the magazine section; you'll probably be surprised and delighted by the wide range of offerings.

If you're interested in finding multicultural films, you'll have to look a little harder. The high cost of film production has resulted in a lack of representation by most people of color and other minorities among producers, directors, and even actors. Some exceptions include African American directors Spike Lee and John Singleton, Asian American directors Wayne Wang and Ang Lee, and Mexican American director Gregory Nava, all of whom offer new perspectives on American life and merit attention from wide audiences. (For a list of feature films focusing on multicultural life and issues, see Appendix B.)

While multicultural films are still relatively scarce among high-budget, Hollywood productions, you can discover a thriving world of independent films (mostly documentaries) by obtaining catalogues from organizations specializing in cross-cultural materials. The National Asian American Telecommunications Association (NAATA), for example, offers a wide variety of films, videos, and audiocassettes that, as the catalogue states, "challenge mainstream notions of Asian-American and Pacific Islander identities." California Newsreel offers an outstanding selection of films on African Americans; an organization called Women Make Movies is the leading distributor nationwide of films and videotapes by women (for further references, see Appendix B).

Multicultural film festivals, which are becoming increasingly widespread and extremely popular, offer another source to explore. Some events, like the annual American Indian Film Festival in San Francisco and the biennial Native American Film and Video Festival in New York City, receive national attention, and many others are springing up in smaller cities and towns for local audiences. These festivals offer the opportunity to view films that often receive limited distribution and may otherwise be difficult to locate.

Of course, the distinction between mainstream and alternative—whether applied to print media, films, or radio and television—can be fuzzy. Some might claim, for example, that *Ms.* magazine has now become mainstream or that responsible investigative reporters in the mainstream press do write "alternative-like" articles. But haggling over definitions is less important than becoming acquainted with the thought-provoking ideas and points of view presented in alternative sources. You can't always find this material at a corner newsstand or grocery store, but it is nonetheless readily available to those who do a bit of searching, and the search will almost always yield unexpected, worthwhile results.

17

Multicultural Backpacking

*Travel is fatal to prejudice, bigotry, and
narrow-mindedness...*
—Mark Twain

One of the joys of living in a multicultural society is the opportunity to travel to other cultures—without leaving the country. Just as the American abroad experiences new sights, foods, languages, and ideas, so does the multicultural traveler at home.

But how, exactly, do you discover multicultural America? Where do you need to go, and what do you need to do when you get there?

Depending on your interests, there are many easy, accessible points of entry. The most appealing, for starters, is probably food. Check your local yellow pages for restaurants that offer ethnic foods. If you live in or near a city, or when you travel to one, do some gastronomical exploration. In addition to Jewish delicatessens and Japanese sushi bars, you'll find Lebanese, Moroccan, Indian, Thai, Greek, and Korean restaurants. If you don't know the difference between Greek *dolmades* (stuffed grape leaves) and *soupa avgolemeno* (egg and lemon soup), ask for help; people are trained to answer questions and are usually pleased to tell you about their menu and to make recommendations.

The same applies to ethnic grocery stores and bakeries. Don't walk past an ethnic food store, whether Korean, Arab, or Indian, without taking a few minutes to stroll up and down the aisles, smelling and examining the offerings; and consider taking a few groceries home (even if you don't recognize what they are).

But don't stop with foods. As you begin to look around, you'll find ethnic shops, art galleries, museums, and places of worship; and you'll learn about festivals, dances, and concerts held in various large and small communities as well as at local colleges and universities. These are usually open to the public (you can often find advertisements of events in the Sunday papers), and visitors are welcome.

If you find yourself in a big metropolitan area, the choices will be virtually endless. Take New York, for example. To find out what's available, look at Mark Leeds's 508-page *Passport's Guide to Ethnic New York*. In Leeds's fourteen chapters on the primary groups, including people of color as well as white ethnic groups (Slavs, Greeks, Scandinavians, English, Dutch), we find an intriguing new world that one could continue to explore for a lifetime.

We learn, for example, that in New York one can find a colorful festival almost any time of the year, whether it's the Festa Italiana, Cherry Blossom Festival, West Indian Carnival, India Festival, Harlem Week, or Great Irish Fair. Museum lovers can delight in the Ukrainian Museum, Black Fashion Museum, Jewish Museum, El Museo Del Barrio, and Chinatown History Museum. Readers can browse at the Polish Book Center, Zen Oriental Book Store, Black Sea Bookstore, and Irish Books and Graphics. Shoppers can find Matryosha dolls at the Russia House, embroidered caftans at Alnoor, or Turkish camel saddles at Sahadi Importing Company. Dancers can learn marimba at the East Harlem Music School, or buy merengue CDs at the Dominican Record Shop.

You can also begin to discover ethnic neighborhoods. You may be familiar with Chinatown but not have much confidence in entering the other communities that exist in many cities and towns, known by such names as Little Athens or Greektown, Koreatown, Little Havana, Spanish Harlem, Little Saigon, Little Poland, Little Ukraine, Little Italy, Little India.

One way to begin your exploration is to sign up for a guided tour. Many cities now offer organized bus or walking tours of ethnic sites and neighborhoods. A company called "Roots of New Orleans," for example, offers a wonderful guided tour of African American heritage in the city—with a lunch of Creole and soul food. Also, tourists' guidebooks increasingly include information on ethnic neighborhoods, and regional tourist offices often offer free literature, such as the "St. Louis Multicultural Guide: Our People, Our Heritage, Our Legacy."

Of course, an ideal way to see a community is as an invited guest. Visiting a home, place of worship, social function, or artistic event with a friend or acquaintance gives you a chance to see life from within the culture, rather than simply as an observer on the outside. In addition to what you may learn about the particular cultural group, you'll experience the important emotions and insights of being in a cultural and ethnic minority, which, for many people, especially whites, may not happen very often.

For the serious multicultural backpacker, there are now guidebooks available to sites of interest across the country. If you're interested in Native Americans, for example, *Discover Indian Reservations USA*, edited by Veronica E. Tiller, gives you information, state by state, on locations and accommodations, cultural institutions, special events, archaeological and historical sites, and recreational opportunities. *Indian America: A Traveler's Companion*, edited by Eagle/Walking Turtle, also provides useful visitor information, with appendices that include a powwow calendar for North America; addresses of Indian-owned stores, museums, and cultural centers; a calendar of all-Indian arts and crafts shows and exhibitions; and an Indian rodeo schedule. And the *Insight Guides: Native America*, edited by John Gattuso, provides fascinating historical and cultural background information to those traveling through Indian country.

Similar guidebooks are currently available for other domestic cultures, including Latino America, the Amish country, Buddhist America, Irish America, and Catholic America (see Appendix A, "Multicultural Travel Guides"). African American travel, in particular, has been flourishing over the past decade as millions of black Americans are discovering their heritage. This new tourism industry, now estimated at $30 billion yearly, focuses on the civil rights movement, jazz, the history of slavery, and black literary history. There are guidebooks to black America, the historic black south, black Washington, black New York, and the Underground Railroad.

Additionally, and not to be missed, are the old faithfuls of multicultural travel, such as the Statue of Liberty and Ellis Island, and the "new faithfuls," including the Los Angeles Museum of Tolerance, the Birmingham Civil Rights Institute, the Holocaust Memorial Museum in Washington, D.C., the National Civil Rights Museum in Memphis, the Japanese American National Museum in Los Angeles, and the Smithsonian Institution's National Museum of the American Indian, scheduled to open in 2006 on the Mall in Washington, D.C.

As Americans realize more and more that the rewards usually associated with foreign travel can also be experienced in one's own backyard, a word of caution is in order. Just as the foreign traveler should be sensitive to other cultures and aware of cultural etiquette, so must the domestic traveler. Certain types of behavior may be inappropriate or offensive, and the traveler needs to be informed about customs and expectations. The *Insight Guides: Native America* includes a section on "How to Behave in Indian Country" that advises visitors not to use insulting terms such as *redskin* or *squaw*, not to take pictures of people without permission, and not to ask questions or interrupt during Indian ceremonies and dances.

Also, there may be some places or occasions when visitors are unwelcome. For example, on Indian reservations access may be prohibited in certain wilderness, archaeological, or religious areas. Often restrictions are posted, but there may be times in your multicultural travels when you are uncertain about whether to proceed—whether, for example, to sit in on a particular religious service. In such cases, it's best to find out first how your presence would be perceived before going forward. Again, the parallel with foreign travel is helpful. There are some risks involved, but, to the informed traveler, the risks are minimized—and they are far outweighed by the benefits.

18

Getting Involved: Do Some Personal Brainstorming

Choose one issue that interests you, figure out how much time you have to devote, and get involved.
— Jimmy Carter

The goal of achieving a more inclusive society implies enormous changes and a great deal of work—to combat bigotry and discrimination, to create greater social and economic justice, to promote civil rights. And armchair multiculturalism will not get the job done. Even if you have never thought of yourself as an activist, this chapter can help you understand that there are ways to become involved that suit your needs, abilities, pocketbook, time constraints, and interests. Once you realize that you have something to contribute and decide that you *want* to contribute, the path to active involvement can be found by doing some personal brainstorming.

Organizational Activism

Let's begin by looking at the possibility of your joining an advocacy organization. For many people, this is the best way to feel a sense of accomplishment, a sense that it's possible to bring about change. In the face of all the problems of a multicultural society, it's easy and tempting to throw up our hands and do nothing. Alone, we feel overwhelmed and powerless. Yet, the moment we join with other like-minded people—the moment we get organized—things don't look nearly as bleak or hopeless.

The good news is that you don't have to create your own organization (unless, of course, you want to). There are hundreds of groups already working for causes linked with multiculturalism. If you're interested in working for civil rights, for example, you might be interested in joining the National Association for the Advancement of Colored People (NAACP), the Anti-Defamation League of B'nai B'rith (ADL), the American Civil Liberties Union (ACLU), or the Southern Poverty Law Center. Many other organizations actively promote women's rights; rights of African, Asian, Latino, and Native Americans; gay and lesbian rights; rights of children and the elderly; and rights of people with disabilities. For a partial listing of such groups, see Appendix C. For more complete information on these and other organizations, consult David Walls's excellent *Activist's Almanac*. Walls provides capsule summaries of the purpose, goals, structure, resources, publications, and services of more than one hundred organizations. By writing to any of these organizations (or consulting their "home pages," as suggested below), you can obtain further background and membership information, and you can inquire as to where the nearest local chapter is and who to contact.

If your interests are more cultural than political, you can join numerous groups that organize and sponsor artistic performances, film and lecture series, and other educational programs. These organizations range widely in purpose, from a group like the Deaf Artists of America, which strives to make the arts more accessible to the deaf and hard of hearing, to the Surmire-Society, intended for enthusiasts of Oriental brush painting. You can also become a member of museums (Museum of African American History), cinema societies (Gay and Lesbian Media Coalition), historical associations (Norwegian American Historical Association), or groups interested in historical preservation (Coordinating Committee for Ellis Island or Crazy Horse Memorial Foundation).

Should you wish to concentrate on issues that are more local in scope, almost every town now has its own human rights, peace, or mediation groups as well as cultural organizations of regional importance. These grassroots efforts are a great way to learn more about the needs of your own community and at the same time broaden your multicultural understanding.

Checkbook Activism

If you don't have the time to join an organization, or if you would rather contribute in some other way, you can lend financial support. Most organizations depend heavily on dues and modest individual contributions, and if you donate enough to be a member, you'll receive regular mailings and information updates.

A relatively new method of supporting organizations financially is the affinity credit card. Generally, the organization you want to support receives one-half to one percent of the total charges to your card. You can also contribute to nonprofit groups through your phone company (see Appendix D).

Another way to put your money to work is by choosing your investments carefully. This can be important not only if you own stocks and bonds, but also if you have a bank account, some type of insurance, or some kind of retirement fund. You now have the option of opening accounts at a variety of minority- and women-owned banks, and you can choose banks that invest in low-income communities and socially responsible causes. In addition, small investors can use a variety of socially responsible mutual funds for general savings and investing as well as for pension plans. (See Appendix D for further information.)

Computer Activism

With new computer technology, you need not leave your keyboard to be a multicultural activist. From the comfort of your home, you can stay up to date on a wide variety of multicultural issues, support relevant legislation, respond to or post your own calls for action, reply to or make inquiries, gain access to news reports that are otherwise unavailable, and take part in lively debates and discussions.

Most of the popular commercial Internet services have "forums" or "conferences" on human rights issues. These are simply networks of people nationwide or worldwide who communicate with each other, sharing information and ideas. You can also join a network more focused on your specialized interests. The largest worldwide network for peace, justice, and environmental activists is the Institute for Global Communications (http://www.igc.org/igc), which offers a family of subnets such as PeaceNet, LaborNet, EcoNet, WomensNet, and ConflictNet. By linking to PeaceNet, for example, you can take part in its forum on racism, which provides not only a wealth of articles, essays, and other information but also contains important calls to action, ranging from sending electronic letters or faxes to supporting candidates or legislation to boycotting companies and products. Other similar specialized networks include SeniorNet for the elderly (http://www.seniornet.org) and TogetherNet (http://www.together.org/orgs/un), which is similar to the PeaceNet and has a direct link to the United Nations.

Also, you can consult the home pages of many of the organizations listed in Appendix C to become a member and obtain additional information.

While you may decide that computer activism is the best route for you, don't hesitate to be active in other ways simultaneously—as a member of an organization, or through donations. The different forms of activism often go together, as, for example, when you are considering organizing a local event. A call for assistance at your computer will bring immediate help and support, and you'll find that you may be in a position to offer assistance to others as well.

19

Multicultural Dilemmas: Mini Case Studies

What we must defend is dialogue.
　　　　　　　　　　　—Albert Camus

This book places its faith in education. As we have seen in previous chapters, we not only have the responsibility in our multicultural society to re-educate ourselves so that we begin to know who our neighbors really are, but we also need to learn and practice new skills. By making this type of education a personal and national priority, we can unquestionably make enormous strides and improve the quality of our lives.

Yet it would be irresponsible to suggest that through learning and goodwill alone we can solve all our problems. Indeed, the more interested and involved you become in multicultural issues, the more you will begin to see that there are no easy answers. Many of the concrete questions we face are so complex and emotion-laden that even among multiculturalists there is little sense of a clear-cut, unwavering response.

To give you a feel for the types of real dilemmas that continue to defy satisfactory solutions, this chapter describes three sample case studies. If you are part of a class, discuss the questions posed in each case study in small groups and try to reach consensus. You can also use the case studies as themes for role plays, with students volunteering to represent various points of view. The readings and other assignments can serve as preparation for the role plays. If you are simply reading this book on your own, you may want to discuss the issues with friends and do some additional research independently. Whatever the case, keep an eye out for how these and other multicultural dilemmas evolve in public thinking and the press.

Note that the first case study is based on an actual event, but the names and a few minor details have been changed. The second case study is not based on one single occurrence, but rather describes a phenomenon observable at many schools and universities. The third case study is factual, based on readers' responses to John Callahan, as reported in the *New York Times Magazine* (7 June 1992).

Multicultural Dilemma 1: Transracial Adoptions: A White Couple Seeks Custody of Two Black Children

In 1994, a white couple, Lisa and Charles Green, took a one-month-old black child, Joshua, into their foster home. Joshua and his older brother, Charles, who is also being cared for by the Greens, had both been given up for adoption by their birth mother. Now the Greens wish to adopt both Joshua, age 3, and Charles, 6, but they have been told by their social worker that this is impossible;

the children need to be placed in black homes to preserve their cultural identity. Over the past few years, the social agency has made some efforts to find an African American family but as yet has not been successful.

The Question: Should the Greens be allowed to adopt Joshua, Charles, or both children, or should further attempts be made to place the children with an African American family?

Background: Nationwide, foster parents care for approximately five hundred thousand children, of whom sixty to one hundred thousand are legally adoptable. Almost half of the adoptable children are minorities, mostly black; however, not enough minority families are available to keep up with the demand for placements (or perhaps they have not been recruited aggressively enough).

With respect to the present legal situation, many states favor the practice of race matching, but a 1995 federal law, the Multiethnic Placement Act, prohibits agencies receiving federal funds from delaying or denying adoptions on the basis of race, color, or nationality. This act also requires states to recruit nonwhite adoptive parents actively and creatively.

Points to Consider before Reaching Your Decision

1. Do you think a child suffers from being placed with parents of a different race or cultural background? How? If there are harmful effects, how might they be minimized?

2. Do you think the child and adoptive family can benefit from transracial and transethnic adoptions? What might possible benefits be?

3. In 1972, the National Association of Black Social Workers declared white adoptions of

black babies to be "cultural genocide." Is there validity to this claim? When and why might transracial adoptions be viewed as exploitation?

4. If you favor matching policies, should there be a time limit on how long agencies may search for a match? If so, how should the time limit be determined?

5. If you favor transracial adoptions, are there ways in which children can be connected with their racial and cultural origins?

6. If race and ethnicity are acceptable criteria, what about religion, social class, and disability? Should, for example, a deaf or blind child be placed with a deaf or blind parent? Are there other possible criteria for matching?

7. How might it affect your thinking if Lisa Green were Latina, Native American, or African American, and her husband Charles were white? What if they were both white but had already adopted an African American or Asian American child?

Further Independent Research or Class Assignments

1. Call your state office on children and families to obtain relevant information on transracial adoptions in your state. How well is the Multiethnic Placement Act working? Are minority families being recruited effectively? If possible, speak with a representative for his or her opinion on transracial adoptions.

2. Find out how your local elected representatives feel about, and have voted on, adoption issues.

Multicultural Dilemma 2: Self-Segregation: Latino Students at a California University Request Their Own Residence Hall

At a large public California university, Latinos make up 7 percent of the population; the remaining students are white (55 percent), Asian (25 percent), African American (5 percent), and international students and others (8 percent). The Latino students feel that they are generally viewed as less competent than other students, in part because others suspect they have gained admission through affirmative action. They have little voice in student government or activities and often feel isolated and uncomfortable. A dormitory facility would, they believe, give them a "home," a place where they can relax, speak Spanish if they wish, and enjoy the company of other Latinos. Also, they believe that by living together they can build their own self-esteem and gradually become more active in the life of the university.

The dean of housing is opposed to the dormitory, since he feels that students who segregate themselves now will never learn to live together after graduation. The president of the university has not made up her mind.

The Question: Should the university administration respond to the Latino students' request by creating a residential facility for them?

Background: In its landmark ruling in 1954, *Brown v. Board of Education*, the Supreme Court decreed that separate education for blacks was inherently unequal, overturning decades of racial segregation and paving the way for integrated schools and a more fully integrated society. Now, over forty years later, many African Americans and other people of color maintain that integration has failed and that emphasis should be put on establishing and enhancing separate schools and separate facilities.

Even at integrated schools and universities, people of color claim their right to have their own organizations, fraternities, and dormitories—and, in some cases, their own yearbooks and proms. Women also feel it is essential to have their own social and political organizations.

Points to Consider before Reaching Your Decision

1. If this dorm is created, what should the policy be regarding who is able to live there?

2. Will a Latino residence hall pave the way for other ethnic, racial, religious, and special interest or "theme" dorms? What "themes" should qualify? What are potential pros and cons of a trend toward separate living facilities?

3. Are there other ways for the Latino students to feel more comfortable at the university, or is the living situation the key element?

4. Do separate residence halls represent a form of discrimination against others? What if there were a residence hall designated for white men (or white women)?

5. How might an ethnic group living in its own dorm increase its sense of isolation on campus? And what are the ways the facility might help students to become more involved in university life?

6. Is it legitimate for students of color in high schools and universities to have their own sororities and fraternities or cultural organizations? How about their own proms, yearbooks, graduation ceremonies, and reunions,

especially if they feel their wishes are not respected by the majority?

Further Independent Research or Class Assignments

1. Research the *Brown v. Board of Education* case.
2. Find out whether separate dormitories (or other separate facilities) exist at your own or a nearby university.
3. Inquire as to how integrated (or segregated) local neighborhoods and schools are.

Multicultural Dilemma 3: Offensive Humor?: Some Upset Readers Demand That Their Local Newspaper Remove John Callahan's Column

John Callahan, syndicated cartoonist and author of an autobiography (*Don't Worry, He Won't Get Too Far on Foot*)[1] as well as numerous books of cartoons, is known for humor that targets disabled people, people of color, and the disadvantaged. Himself a quadriplegic, Callahan rejects the idea that there are limits to his humor. He is tired of others speaking for the disabled and reserves the right to laugh at himself and others like him. His loyal fans, including many people with disabilities, believe that his humor can actually liberate people and help them cope with their pain.

Callahan's critics see his humor as hurtful and dehumanizing. Some readers were especially upset by a cartoon entitled "The Alzheimer Hoedown," which shows confused couples at a square dance, milling about and unable to remember the

---

[1] John Callahan, *Don't Worry, He Won't Get Too Far on Foot* (New York: Random House, 1990).

caller's instructions to "return to the girl that you just left." A flood of letters to some of the papers that run Callahan's cartoons expressed anger about another cartoon depicting a black beggar on a street corner with a sign reading, "Please help me. I am blind and black but not musical."

The Question: If you were on the editorial board of a newspaper, would you recommend cancelling Callahan's column in light of your readers' protests?

Points to Consider before Reaching Your Decision

1. To what extent does Callahan's own disability allow him freedom to poke fun at quadriplegics? At people with other disabilities? At anyone he wishes?

2. Obtain a book of Callahan's cartoons and analyze your own reactions. What do you find funny, offensive, or distasteful, and why?

3. The American Civil Liberties Union of Oregon awarded Callahan its Free Expression Award in 1991. How important is it to you that this type of free expression be protected? Are there circumstances under which humor should be censored?

4. If a person hears what seems to be inappropriate ethnic jokes or cultural humor in a group, what do you think she or he should do?

5. When faced with criticism, Callahan usually relies on the simple defense that his cartoons are funny. Is this a legitimate defense?

Further Independent Research
or Class Assignments

1. Read Callahan's autobiography.

2. Try to find information on stand-up comedian Chris Fonseca, who has cerebral palsy and uses his disability as part of his routine.

3. Look into one or more types of ethnic humor and try to characterize the humor. What, for example, is typical of African American, Jewish, gay and lesbian, Latino, or Native American humor?

As these three case studies demonstrate, the dilemmas in a multicultural society can be difficult, painful, and controversial. Although there are no decisions or solutions that will fully satisfy everyone, we may be able, by means of open discussion and a willingness to compromise, to devise solutions that are at least acceptable to most parties. These solutions should never be regarded as permanent or final; they should always be reviewed and revised in the search for better answers.

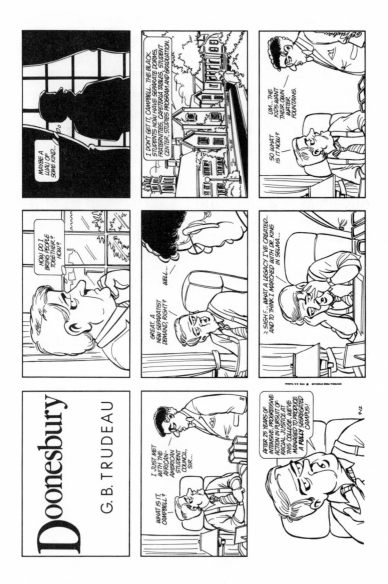

20

Multicultural Success Stories: People Like Ourselves

> *Darkness cannot drive out darkness; only light can do that. Hate cannot drive out hate; only love can do that.*
> —Martin Luther King, Jr.

The many topics we have addressed—racism, discrimination, prejudice, hate crimes—can make for heavy reading and heavy-heartedness. While the history of our country gives us ample reason to despair at our inability to deliver on the promise of "liberty and justice for all," the unnoticed actions of millions of people every day can restore one's faith.

Success stories can be found everywhere, and they are often not grandiose or well remembered. But they do matter, and, taken together, they have the potential to change the way we live.

In this chapter we will look at two noteworthy success stories, noteworthy because they originated with private citizens who had the courage to act in accordance with their beliefs. They are intentionally not the stories of heroes (of well-known, distinguished political or civic leaders) but rather of ordinary human beings.

Success Story 1: "Not in Our Town"

In Billings, Montana (pop. 84,000), a series of incidents instigated by white supremacist groups—including distributing hate literature, vandalizing a Jewish cemetery, and defacing the home of a Native American woman—culminated in an occurrence that roused the town to action. On December 2, 1993, a cinder block was thrown through the window of a Jewish family's home, leaving shattered glass on a child's bed. The window had been decorated with a menorah, the nine-branched candelabrum symbolic of the Jewish holiday of Hanukkah. The local paper subsequently quoted Tammie Schnitzer, the child's mother, as saying that she was advised by authorities to remove the menorah, but she was reluctant to do so, since she would not know how to explain this to her child.

A townswoman, who recalled the story of the Danes' reaction to the Nazi order that Danish Jews wear prominently displayed Stars of David, realized that community members needed to show their solidarity with the Schnitzer family. Remembering that the king of Denmark and other Danes also wore yellow stars to confuse the Nazis, she worked through her church to distribute paper menorahs, and the local paper published a full-page illustration of a menorah for people to cut out. Ultimately, windows were decorated with three to four thousand menorahs (some say as many as ten thousand), in a town with only forty-eight Jewish families. And a sports equipment store proclaimed in large letters on its outdoor display sign: "Not in Our Town! No hate. No violence. Peace on earth."

When the violence and threats continued, townspeople continued to resist in quiet but determined ways: a vigil, for example, was held in the dark outside a Hanukkah service. In the new year, tension persisted, since the hate groups were still active, but there were fewer, more scattered incidents. Though the struggle is far from over, Billings citizens did achieve an important victory, as expressed by the chief of police, Wayne Inman: "There was not silence. There was community outrage, saying, 'If you harass and intimidate one member of this community, you are attacking all of us.'"[1]

For more complete information on this remarkable story, see the article, "Their Finest Minute" (*New York Times Magazine*, 3 July 1994), or order the documentary *Not in Our Town* (tel. 800-358-3000). These sources provide a close look at the soul-searching that took place in Billings and offer insights into complex questions: What does it take for people to mobilize? What are the risks? What type of leadership is needed? How does a community sustain its commitment to tolerance?

Using the videotape as an educational tool, Oregon Governor John Kitzhaber and Portland Mayor Vera Katz declared the first week of January, 1996, as "Not In Our Town Week." During this week, the documentary was broadcast on Oregon Public Broadcasting, followed by an interview with Police Chief Inman and other spokespeople. Viewings were also held at numerous locations in five cities, followed by discussions focusing on

---

[1] Tom Lackety, "Montana Town Refuses to Accept Hate Attacks," *Oregonian*, 20 February 1994.

how Oregonians can oppose hate crime in their own towns.

A follow-up video, *Not in Our Town II* (also available from above phone listing), shows how Americans are fighting back against local hate crimes. Bloomington, Illinois, for example, has adopted "Not in Our Town" as its motto and established a neighborhood watch program to stop hate violence. Various communities throughout the South have mobilized to protect African American churches from arson, and volunteers in other towns have helped to rebuild churches that were destroyed. A "Not in Our Town" home page (http://www.igc.org/an/niot) encourages people around the country to become active in their own communities.

Success Story 2: "Deaf President Now" at Gallaudet University

In March, 1988, students at Gallaudet University, a nationally renowned university for the deaf, changed forever the way people with disabilities are viewed by others—and the way they view themselves. Facing the opportunity of electing the first deaf president in the school's 124-year history, thousands of students, faculty, staff, and alumni, wearing blue and yellow buttons that read "DEAF PRESIDENT NOW," held a rally in support of choosing one of the two deaf finalists for the position. A third finalist was not deaf. One of the speakers at the rally, Professor Allen Sussman, made the powerful point: "This is an historical event. You could call this the first deaf civil rights activity."[2] Many in the audience were thus made

---

[2] Joseph P. Shapiro, *No Pity: People with Disabilities Forging a New Civil Rights Movement* (New York: Random House, 1993), 77.

aware for the first time of the link between the treatment of the deaf and civil rights.

A few days later, the university board announced its decision to appoint the lone hearing candidate, Elisabeth Zinser, as president. The hearing chairwoman of the board, Jane Spilman, was reported as offering the rationale that "deaf people are incapable of functioning in a hearing world,"[3] though she later denied having made this statement. The campus revolted. During the following week, students boycotted classes, received wide coverage in the national media, gained the support of deaf organizations and leaders across the country, and organized marches on the White House and Capitol. Refusing to recognize Zinser as the new president, they demanded (1) that she resign and that a deaf president be named, (2) that Spilman also resign, and (3) that a majority of deaf members be named to the board.

One week after the protests had begun, all the demands were met and I. Jordan King, the popular dean of arts and sciences who had become deaf as a young adult, was named the university's first deaf president.

By refusing to accept limitations imposed upon them by a hearing world, the Gallaudet community gave powerful impetus to the disability rights movement across the country. They instilled a new sense of pride in the deaf community. And they realized their potential to challenge the system and bring about meaningful change.

For further information about the Gallaudet story, see the relevant sections in Harlan Lane's *The Mask of Benevolence: Disabling the Deaf Com-*

---

[3] Ibid., 78.

munity, Joseph P. Shapiro's *No Pity,* and Oliver Sacks *Seeing Voices: A Journey into the World of the Deaf.* These authors provide an inside view of both the emotional intensity and political consequences of the Gallaudet revolution.

The Billings and Gallaudet stories remind us that ordinary people can stand up for themselves, and for each other, to create a more just and humane society. And these are only two of many such success stories that could be told. Take, for example, Oseola McCarty, an eighty-seven-year-old African American woman from Hattiesburg, Mississippi, who, having spent a lifetime washing laundry, donated a $150,000 scholarship to a local university so that young African Americans could receive the education she never had. Or Marilyn Hamilton, who, having become a paraplegic after a hang glider accident, reinvented the wheelchair, making a bulky, unattractive object into a flashy, lightweight, neon-colored symbol of pride. Or the many thousands of residents of interracial communities who are committing themselves and their families every day to integrated living.

If we recognize and focus on these stories, they can serve as needed antidotes to the well-publicized tales of cultural misunderstandings, conflicts, and animosity so often heard. However small the individual successes may seem, they serve as examples of the positive role that any one of us can play in achieving human dignity in our multicultural society.

21

Looking to the Future: A Global View

America's main role in the new world order is not as a military superpower, but as a multicultural superpower.
—Federico Mayor Zaragoza,
Director General of UNESCO

While the issues and controversies discussed in this book may seem to be uniquely American, there is virtually no corner of the earth untouched by multiculturalism. Other societies and nations are facing their own multicultural issues, and many are becoming acutely aware of the need for new approaches and new ideas.

Unfortunately, the most visible evidence of multiculturalism in the world is conflict. In the mid-1990s, there were at any given time as many as fifty ethnic and religious wars being waged, many of them long-standing struggles: between Catholics and Protestants in Northern Ireland; Jews and Arabs in Israel; blacks and whites in South Africa; and Serbs, Muslims, and Croats in

Bosnia. We are all familiar with the monumental events surrounding the breakup of the former Soviet Union, and we know of the disastrous ethnic clashes between Tutsis and Hutus in Rwanda and Burundi. While some of these conflicts may seem far away, we are also following the struggles of our neighbor Canada, a long-established democracy, as it threatens to break apart under pressure from both Quebec separatists and the Western provinces.

This threat of breaking down into smaller and smaller groups seems to have no foreseeable end. How large, or different, should an ethnic or religious group have to be to qualify for its own nation? Should the three million Basques have the freedom to create their own independent state between Spain and France? Should the Kurds be able to create their own country? What about the fact that many of the independent states of the former Soviet Union are themselves multiethnic societies, marked by striking cultural, class, and religious differences? And closer to home, what about the Native Hawaiians, who are engaged in a serious struggle for sovereignty or self-rule?

Clearly, disintegration into separate, homogeneous groups is not a viable solution on any grounds, whether geographical, political, or moral. New and rapidly changing immigration patterns, in particular, make it impossible to see the world in anything but multicultural terms. For example, entire new populations of Muslims (ten to thirteen million) from Asia, Turkey, and North Africa are rapidly transforming the social and political landscapes of Western European countries. Peoples of differing beliefs and backgrounds in Europe and elsewhere have no choice but to find new ways to live together, within the boundaries of their own societies as well as across national lines.

Moreover, as we have seen, the conflicts and discrimination marring the world's cultural landscapes are not based solely on differences in religion, ethnicity, or race. In many societies, people with disabilities suffer severe discrimination. Official attitudes toward homosexuality in most countries of the world are hostile, ranging from subtle repression to outright persecution. And burgeoning as well as ongoing struggles for equal rights for women are taking place across the globe.

Where are the models for a new world order? What is our vision of the future? What solutions are being attempted? Some people place their hopes on new forms of international diplomacy, with bodies such as the United Nations playing a more active and effective role in dispute prevention and resolution. Similarly, some call for the establishment of an international tribunal specifically for the purpose of hearing grievances by ethnic minorities in various countries. Some find inspiration in the European Union, which is indeed a farsighted experiment that runs counter to the global trend toward increased factionalism.

Undoubtedly, the United States has a role to play in creating the multicultural order or disorder of the coming century. The tasks are formidable. Will we be able to muster the enormous financial and human resources needed to create a new society closer in practice to our founding principles? How can we ensure that *all* the people are included in the decision-making process? Are we prepared to rededicate ourselves to combating chronic poverty, undereducation, criminality, and homelessness among large segments of our multicultural population? By addressing our problems at home and improving the lives of our own citizens, we will, at the same time, have an unprecedented opportunity to exercise moral leadership in the global community.

Appendix A

Suggestions for Further Reading

General References on Multiculturalism

Allport, Gordon. *The Nature of Prejudice.* Cambridge, MA: Addison-Wesley, 1979.

Anderson, Bonnie S., and Judith P. Zinsser. *A History of Their Own: Women in Europe.* 2 vols. New York: Harper and Row, 1988.

Atlas, James. *Battle of the Books: The Curriculum Debate in America.* New York: W. W. Norton, 1990.

Auerbach, Susan, ed. *Encyclopedia of Multiculturalism.* 6 vols. New York: Marshall Cavendish, 1994.

Aufderheide, Pat, ed. *Beyond PC: Toward a Politics of Understanding.* Saint Paul, MN: Graywolf Press, 1992.

Banks, James A. *Teaching Strategies for Ethnic Studies.* 5th ed. Boston: Allyn & Bacon, 1991.

Bawer, Bruce. *A Place at the Table: The Gay Individual in American Society.* New York: Simon and Schuster, 1993.

Bell, Derrick. *Faces at the Bottom of the Well: The Permanence of Racism.* New York: HarperCollins, 1992.

Berman, Paul, ed. *Debating P.C.: The Controversy over Political Correctness on College Campuses.* New York: Dell, 1992.

Bernstein, Richard. *Dictatorship of Virtue: Multiculturalism and the Battle for America's Future.* New York: Alfred A. Knopf, 1994.

Bloom, Allan. *The Closing of the American Mind: How Higher Education Has Failed Democracy and Impoverished the Souls of Today's Students.* New York: Simon and Schuster, 1987.

Borjas, George J. "The New Economics of Immigration." *Atlantic Monthly,* November 1996.

Bowser, Benjamin P., Gale S. Auletta, and Terry Jones. *Confronting Diversity Issues on Campus.* Newbury Park, CA: Sage, 1993.

Brimelow, Peter. *Alien Nation: Common Sense about America's Immigration Disaster.* New York: Random House, 1995.

Brown, Dee. *Bury My Heart at Wounded Knee: An Indian History of the American West.* New York: Henry Holt, 1970.

Callahan, John. *Don't Worry, He Won't Get Too Far on Foot.* New York: Random House, 1990.

Carter, Stephen L. *Reflections of an Affirmative Action Baby.* New York: HarperCollins, 1991.

Chideya, Farai. *Don't Believe the Hype: Fighting Cultural Misinformation about African-Americans.* New York: Penguin Books, 1995.

Ch'maj, Betty E. M., ed. *Multicultural America: A Resource Book for Teachers of Humanities and American Studies.* Lanham, MD: University Press of America, 1993.

Crawford, James. *Hold Your Tongue: Bilingualism and the Politics of "English Only."* Reading, MA: Addison-Wesley, 1992.

————, ed. *Language Loyalties: A Source Book on the Official English Controversy.* Chicago: University of Chicago Press, 1992.

Dalton, Harlon L. *Racial Healing: Confronting the Fear between Blacks and Whites.* New York: Doubleday, 1995.

Daniels, Harvey A., ed. *Not Only English: Affirming America's Multicultural Heritage.* Urbana, IL: National Council of Teachers of English, 1990.

DeMott, Benjamin. *The Trouble with Friendship: Why Americans Can't Think Straight about Race.* New York: Atlantic Monthly Press, 1995.

D'Souza, Dinesh. *Illiberal Education: The Politics of Race and Sex on Campus.* New York: Vintage, 1991.

Eddy, Robert F., ed. *Reflections on Multiculturalism.* Yarmouth, ME: Intercultural Press, 1996.

Ezekiel, Raphael S. *The Racist Mind: Portraits of American Neo-Nazis and Klansmen.* New York: Penguin, 1995.

Fahy, Una. *How to Make the World a Better Place for Gays and Lesbians.* New York: Warner Books, 1995.

Fish, Stanley. *There's No Such Thing as Free Speech and It's a Good Thing Too.* New York: Oxford University Press, 1994.

Ford, Clyde W. *We Can All Get Along: 50 Steps You Can Take to Help End Racism.* New York: Dell, 1994.

Fowler, Sandra M., and Monica G. Mumford. *Intercultural Sourcebook: Cross-Cultural Training and Methods.* vol. 1. Yarmouth, ME: Intercultural Press, 1995.

Fraser, Steven, ed. *The Bell Curve Wars: Race, Intelligence, and the Future of America.* New York: HarperCollins, 1995.

Freire, Paulo. *Pedagogy of the Oppressed.* New York: Continuum, 1970.

Funderburg, Lise. *Black, White, Other: Biracial Americans Talk about Race and Identity.* New York: William Morrow, 1994.

Gates, Henry Louis, Jr. *Loose Canons: Notes on the Culture Wars.* New York: Oxford University Press, 1992.

Gates, Henry Louis, Jr., and Nellie Y. McKay, eds. *The Norton Anthology of African American Literature.* New York: W. W. Norton, 1996.

Gilligan, Carol. *In a Different Voice: Psychological Theory and Women's Development.* Cambridge: Harvard University Press, 1982.

Gochenour, Theodore. *Beyond Experience: The Experiential Approach to Cross-Cultural Education.* 2d ed. Yarmouth, ME: Intercultural Press, 1993.

Graff, Gerald. *Beyond the Culture Wars: How Teaching the Conflicts Can Revitalize American Education.* New York: W. W. Norton, 1992.

Guinier, Lani. *The Tyranny of the Majority: Fundamental Fairness in Representative Democracy.* New York: Macmillan, 1994.

Hacker, Andrew. *Two Nations: Black and White, Separate, Hostile, Unequal.* New York: Scribner's, 1992.

Herbst, Philip H. *The Color of Words: An Encyclopædic Dictionary of Ethnic Bias in the United States.* Yarmouth, ME: Intercultural Press, 1997.

Hirsch, E. D., Jr. *Cultural Literacy: What Every American Needs to Know.* New York: Random House, 1987.

Hirsch, E. D., Jr., Joseph F. Klett, and James Trefil, eds. *The Dictionary of Cultural Literacy.* Boston: Houghton Mifflin, 1988.

Hollinger, David A. *Postethnic America: Beyond Multiculturalism.* New York: HarperCollins, 1995.

Howe, Irving, and Kenneth Libo. *How We Lived: A Documentary History of Immigrant Jews in America 1880-1930.* New York: Richard Marek, 1979.

Jacoby, Russell. *Dogmatic Wisdom: How the Culture Wars Divert America and Distract Education.* New York: Doubleday, 1994.

Katz, Judith. *White Awareness: Handbook for Anti-Racism Training.* Norman, OK: University of Oklahoma Press, 1978.

Kivel, Paul. *Uprooting Racism: How White People Can Work for Racial Justice.* Philadelphia: New Society Publishers, 1996.

Kochman, Thomas. *Black and White Styles in Conflict.* Chicago: University of Chicago Press, 1981.

Kohls, Robert L., and John M. Knight. *Developing Intercultural Awareness: A Cross-Cultural Training Handbook.* 2d. ed. Yarmouth, ME: Intercultural Press, 1994.

Kovacs, Edna. *Writing across Cultures: A Handbook on Writing Poetry and Lyrical Prose.* Hillsboro, OR: Blue Heron, 1994.

Lane, Harlan. *The Mask of Benevolence: Disabling the Deaf Community.* New York: Random House, 1992.

Lefkowitz, Mary. *Not out of Africa: How Afrocentrism Became an Excuse to Teach Myth as History.* New York: HarperCollins, 1996.

Levin, Jack, and Jack McDevitt. *Hate Crimes: The Rising Tide of Bigotry and Bloodshed.* New York: Plenum Press, 1993.

Levine, Lawrence W. *The Opening of the American Mind: Canons, Culture, and History.* Boston: Beacon Press, 1996.

Marcus, Eric. *Is It a Choice?: Answers to 300 of the Most Frequently Asked Questions about Gays and Lesbians.* New York: HarperCollins, 1993.

Matsuda, Mari J., Charles R. Lawrence III, Richard Delgado, and Kimberlè Williams Crenshaw. *Words That Wound: Critical Race Theory, Assaultive Speech and the First Amendment.* Boulder, CO: Westview Press, 1993.

McIntosh, Peggy. *Interactive Phases of Curricular and Personal Re-Vision with Regard to Race.* Working Paper No. 219. Wellesley, MA: Wellesley College Center for Research on Women, 1990.

———. *White Privilege and Male Privilege: A Personal Account of Coming to See Correspondences through Work in Women's Studies.* Working Paper No. 189. Wellesley, MA: Wellesley College Center for Research on Women, 1988.

Mills, Nicolaus, ed. *Arguing Immigration: The Debate over the Changing Face of America.* New York: Simon and Schuster, 1994.

————. *Debating Affirmative Action: Race, Gender, Ethnicity, and the Politics of Inclusion.* New York: Dell, 1994.

Sacks, Oliver. *Seeing Voices: A Journey into the World of the Deaf.* Berkeley, CA: University of California Press, 1989.

Samovar, Larry, and Richard E. Porter. *Intercultural Communication: A Reader.* 8th ed. Belmont, CA: Wadsworth, 1996.

Schlesinger, Arthur, Jr. *The Disuniting of America: Reflections on a Multicultural Society.* New York: W. W. Norton, 1992.

Seelye, H. Ned, ed. *Experiential Activities for Intercultural Learning.* vol. 1. Yarmouth, ME: Intercultural Press, 1996.

Shapiro, Joseph P. *No Pity: People with Disabilities Forging a New Civil Rights Movement.* New York: Random House, 1993.

Shorris, Earl. *Latinos: A Biography of the People.* New York: W. W. Norton, 1992.

Simonson, Rick, and Scott Walker, eds. *The Graywolf Annual 5: Multicultural Literacy, Opening the American Mind.* Saint Paul, MN: Graywolf Press, 1988.

Sowell, Thomas. *Ethnic America: A History.* New York: HarperCollins, 1981.

Steele, Shelby. *The Content of Our Character.* New York: St. Martin's Press, 1990.

Takaki, Ronald. *A Different Mirror: A History of Multicultural America.* Boston: Little, Brown, 1993.

————. *Strangers from a Different Shore: A History of Asian Americans.* Boston: Little, Brown, 1989.

Tannen, Deborah. *You Just Don't Understand: Men and Women in Conversation.* New York: Ballantine, 1991.

Vicoli, Rudolph J., et al., eds. *Gale Encyclopedia of Multicultural America.* 2 vols. Detroit: Gale Research, 1995.

Walker, Samuel. *Hate Speech: The History of an American Controversy.* Lincoln, NE: University of Nebraska Press, 1994.

Walls, David. *The Activist's Almanac: The Concerned Citizen's Guide to the Leading Advocacy Organizations in America.* New York: Simon and Schuster, 1993.

Waters, Mary C. *Ethnic Options: Choosing Identities in America.* Berkeley, CA: University of California Press, 1990.

West, Cornel. *Race Matters.* Boston: Beacon Press. 1993.

Wicker, Tom. *Tragic Failure: Racial Integration in America.* New York: William Morrow, 1996.

Williamson, Chitton, Jr. *The Immigration Mystique: America's False Conscience.* New York: HarperCollins, 1996.

Wilson, John K. *The Myth of Political Correctness: The Conservative Attack on Higher Education.* Durham, NC: Duke University Press, 1995.

Zinn, Howard. *A People's History of the United States.* New York: HarperCollins, 1980.

Multicultural Travel Guides

Biondi, Joann, and James Haskins. *Hippocrene USA Guide to Black New York.* New York: Hippocrene Books, 1993.

Blockson, Charles. *Hippocrene Guide to the Underground Railroad.* New York: Hippocrene Books, 1994.

Chase, Henry. *In Their Footsteps: The American Visions Guide to African-American Heritage Sites.* New York: Henry Holt, 1994.

Chernofsky, Ellen, ed., *Traveling Jewish in America: The Complete Guide for Business and Pleasure.* Lodi, NJ: Wandering You Press, 1991.

Christian-Meyer, Patricia. *Catholic America: Self-Renewal Centers and Retreats.* Santa Fe, NM: John Muir Publications, 1989.

Collins, Andrew. *Fodor's Gay Guide to the USA: The Most Comprehensive Guide for Gay and Lesbian Travelers.* New York: Fodor's Travel Publications, 1996.

Demeter, Richard. *Irish America: The Historical Travel Guide.* Pasadena, CA: Cranford Press, 1995.

Eagle/Walking Turtle. *Indian America: A Traveler's Companion.* Santa Fe, NM: John Muir Publications, 1991.

Fitzpatrick, Sandra, and Maria Goodwin. *Black Washington: Places and Events of Historical and Cultural Significance.* New York: Hippocrene Books, 1993.

Galazka, Jacek, and Albert Juszczak. *Polish Heritage Travel Guide to the USA and Canada.* New York: Hippocrene Books, 1992.

Gattuso, John, ed. *Insight Guides: Native America.* Boston, MA: Houghton Mifflin, 1993.

Haskins, James, and Joann Biondi. *Hippocrene USA Guide to the Historic Black South.* New York: Hippocrene Books, 1993.

Hintz, Martin. *Passport's Guide to Ethnic New Orleans*. Lincolnwood, IL: Passport Books, 1995.

Jones, Oscar, and Joy Jones. *USA Guide to Historic Hispanic America*. New York: Hippocrene Books, 1993.

Leeds, Mark. *Passport's Guide to Ethnic New York*. Lincolnwood, IL: Passport Books, 1996.

Lindberg, Richard. *Passport's Guide to Ethnic Chicago*. Lincolnwood, IL: Passport Books, 1993.

Malone, Russell. *Hippocrene USA Guide to Irish America*. New York: Hippocrene Books, 1994.

McCarthy, Kevin. *Black Florida*. New York: Hippocrene Books, 1995.

Minear, Tish, and Janet Limon. *Discover Native America: Arizona, Colorado, New Mexico and Utah*. New York: Hippocrene Books, 1995.

Morreale, Don, ed. *Buddhist America: Centers, Retreats, Practices*. Santa Fe, NM: John Muir Publications, 1988.

Postal, Bernard, and Lionel Koppman. *Jewish Landmarks of New York: A Travel Guide and History*. New York: Fleet Press, 1978.

Sher, Lynn, and Jurate Kazickas. *Susan B. Anthony Slept Here: A Guide to American Women's Landmarks*. New York: Times Books, 1994.

Simpson, Bill. *Guide to the Amish Country*. 2d ed. Gretna, LA: Pelican Publications, 1995.

Thum, Marcella. *Hippocrene USA Guide to Black America*. New York: Hippocrene Books, 1993.

Tiller, Veronica E., ed. *Discover Indian Reservations USA: A Visitor's Welcome Guide*. Denver, CO: Council Publications, 1992.

Zibart, Eve, Muriel Stevens, and Terell Vermont. *The Unofficial Guide to Ethnic Cuisine and Dining in America*. New York: MacMillan Travel, 1996.

Appendix B

Recommended Feature Films and List of Distributors

African American

Boyz N the Hood
The Color Purple
Crooklyn
Do the Right Thing
Get on the Bus
Ghosts of Mississippi
Glory
Hoop Dreams
Jungle Fever
The Long Walk Home
Malcolm X
Mississippi Burning
Rosewood
A Soldier's Story
Straight out of Brooklyn
To Kill a Mockingbird
*Waiting to Exhale
White Man's Burden

---

*film appears in more than one category

Latino/Hispanic

Ballad of Gregorio Cortez
Born in East L.A.
Break of Dawn
El Norte
La Bamba
Lone Star
Mi Familia
Milagro Beanfield War
Mi Vida Loca
The Perez Family
Salt of the Earth
Stand and Deliver

Asian American

Alamo Bay
Combination Platter
Come See the Paradise
Dim Sum
Double Happiness (Canada)
Eat a Bowl of Tea
A Great Wall
Joy Luck Club
Masala (Canada)
Picture Bride
Rhapsody in August
A Thousand Pieces of Gold
*Wedding Banquet

Immigrants

The Big Night
Far and Away
Green Card
Heaven and Earth
Mississippi Masala
Moscow on the Hudson

American Indian

Black Robe (Canada)
Dance Me Outside (Canada)
Dances with Wolves
Geronimo: An American Legend
Incident at Oglala
Last of the Mohicans
Pocahontas
Powwow Highway
Thunderheart
Where the Spirit Lives

Women

Beaches
*Fried Green Tomatoes
Hannah and Her Sisters
Heidi Chronicles
How to Make an American Quilt
Julia
A League of Their Own
Little Women
Manny and Lo
9 to 5
Spitfire Grill
Steel Magnolias
Strangers in Good Company (Canada)
Thelma and Louise
An Unmarried Woman
*Waiting to Exhale

Homosexuality

Birdcage
Boys on the Side
Desert Heart
Go Fish
The Incredibly True Story of Two Girls in Love

Lianna
 Longtime Companion
 Personal Best
 Philadelphia
*Wedding Banquet

Elderly

 Cocoon
 Foxfire
*Fried Green Tomatoes
 Going in Style
 Harry and Tonto
 On Golden Pond
 Trip to Bountiful
 Whales of August

Disabilities

 Awakenings
 Children of a Lesser God
 Forrest Gump
 Lorenzo's Oil
 The Miracle Worker
 Mr. Holland's Opus
 Mr. Jones
 One Flew over the Cuckoo's Nest
 The Other Side of the Mountain
 Passion Fish
 Rain Man
 Regarding Henry
 Road to Galveston
 The Waterdance
 What's Eating Gilbert Grape

Religion

 Avalon
 The Chosen
 Crossing Delancey

Friendly Persuasion
Moonstruck
Not without My Daughter
School Ties
River Runs through It
A Stranger among Us
Witness

Class

Coal Miner's Daughter
Metropolitan
Norma Rae
Rocky
Trading Places

Major Distributors of Cross-Cultural Documentaries

Bullfrog Films, Inc.
   Olney, PA 19547
   (215) 779-8226

California Newsreel
   149 9th St., Room 420
   San Francisco, CA 94103
   (414) 621-6196

Facets Multimedia Center
   1517 West Fullerton Ave.
   Chicago, IL 60614
   (312) 281-9075; (800) 331-6197

Filmakers Library
   124 E. 40th St., Suite 901
   New York, NY 10016
   (212) 808-4980

First Run/Icarus
   153 Waverly Place, 6th Floor
   New York, NY 10014
   (800) 876-1710

Griggs Productions
302 23rd Ave.
San Francisco, CA 94121
(415) 668-4200

Home Film Festival
P.O. Box 2032
Scranton, PA 18501
(800) 258-3456

Intercultural Press
P.O. Box 700
Yarmouth, ME 04096
(207) 846-5168

Mobility International USA
P.O. Box 3551
Eugene, OR 97403
(503) 343-1284

NAATA/Crosscurrent Media
346 9th St., 2nd Floor
San Francisco, CA 94103
(415) 552-9550

NAFSA: Association of International Educators
1875 Connecticut Ave., NW, Suite 1000
Washington, DC 20009-5728
(202) 462-4811

National Film Board of Canada
1251 Avenue of the Americas, 16th Floor
New York, NY 10020
(212) 586-5131

Native American Public Broadcasting Consortium
P.O. Box 83111
1800 North 33rd St.
Lincoln, NE 68501
(402) 472-3522

PBS Video
    1320 Braddock Place
    Alexandria, VA 22314
    (800) 424-7963

Third World Newsreel
    335 W. 38th St., 5th Floor
    New York, NY 10018
    (212) 947-9227

University of California Extension Media Center
    (UCEMC)
    2176 Shattuck Ave.
    Berkeley, CA 94704
    (510) 642-0460

University of Minnesota Film and Video Service
    1313 5th St. S.E., Suite 108
    Minneapolis, MN 55414
    (800) 542-0013 (Minnesota);
    (800) 547-8251 (out of state)

Women Make Movies
    462 Broadway, Suite 500 C
    New York, NY 10013
    (212) 925-0606

Appendix C

List of Advocacy
Groups and Organizations

Alaska Federation of Natives
411 West 4th Ave., Suite 310
Anchorage, AK 99501

American-Arab Anti-Discrimination Committee (ADC)
4201 Connecticut Ave. NW, Suite 5000
Washington, DC 20008
(202) 244-2990
http://www/adc.org/adc

American Association of Retired Persons (AARP)
601 E St. NW
Washington, DC 20049
(202) 434-2277
http://www.aarp.org

American Civil Liberties Union
132 W. 43rd St.
New York, NY 10036
(212) 944-9800
http://www/aclu.org

American Disability Association
2121 8th Ave. N., Suite 1623
Birmingham, AL 35203
(205) 322-3030

American Indian Movement (AIM)
710 Clayton St., Apt. 1
San Francisco, CA 94117

Amnesty International USA
322 8th Ave.
New York, NY 10001
(212) 807-8400
http://www.amnesty-usa.org

Anti-Defamation League of B'nai B'rith (ADL)
823 United Nations Plaza
New York, NY 10017
(212) 490-2525
http://www/bnaibrith.org

**Asian-American Legal Defense
and Education Fund**
99 Hudson St.
New York, NY 10013
(212) 966-5932

**Association of Asian Indians in America
(AAIA)**
300 Clover St.
Rochester, NY 14610
(716) 288-3874

Center for Democratic Renewal
P.O. Box 50469
Atlanta, GA 30302
(404) 221-0025
http://www.publiceye.org/pra/cdr.html

Center for Immigrants' Rights
48 St. Marks Place
New York, NY 10003
(212) 505-6890

Children's Defense Fund (CDF)
25 E St. NW
Washington, DC 20001
(202) 628-8787
http://www.childrensdefense.org

Chinese for Affirmative Action
17 Walter U. Lum Place
San Francisco, CA 94108
(415) 274-6750
http://www.emf.net/%7Echeetham/gchion-1.html

Cuban American Legal Defense and Education Fund
2119 Webster St.
Fort Wayne, IN 46802
(219) 745-5421

Cultural Survival
96 Mt. Auburn St.'
Cambridge, MA 02138
(617) 441-5400
http://www.cs.org

Disability Rights Education and Defense Fund, Inc.
2212 6th St.
Berkeley, CA 94710
(415) 644-2555

English Plus Information Clearinghouse (EPIC)
200 I St. NE
Washington, DC 20002

Gray Panthers
2025 Pennsylvania Ave. NW
Washington, DC 20006
(202) 466-3132

Habitat for Humanity International
Habitat and Church Streets
Americus, GA 31709
(912) 924-6935
http://www.habitat.org

Human Rights Watch
485 5th Ave.
New York, NY 10007
(212) 972-8400

International Society for Intercultural Education, Training, and Research (SIETAR)
808 17th St. NW, No. 200
Washington, DC 20006
(202) 466-7883

Interracial Family and Social Alliance (IFSA)
P.O. Box 35109
Dallas, TX 75235
(214) 559-6929

Japanese American Citizens League
1765 Sutter St.
San Francisco, CA 94115
(415) 921-5225

Lambda Legal Defense and Education Fund
666 Broadway, 12th Floor
New York, NY 10012
(212) 995-8585
http://www.qrd.org/qrd/orgs/LLDEF

League of United Latin American Citizens (LULAC)
221 N. Kansas, Suite 1211
El Paso, TX 79901
(915) 577-0726
http://www.mundo.com/lulac.html

**Mexican American Legal Defense
and Education Fund**
634 S. Spring St., 11th Floor
Los Angeles, CA 90014
(213) 629-2512

**National Alliance against Racist and
Political Oppression (NAARPO)**
11 John St., Room 202
New York, NY 10038
(212) 406-3330

**National Association for the
Advancement of Colored People (NAACP)**
4805 Mount Hope Dr.
Baltimore, MD 21215
(410) 358-8900
http://www.naacp.org

**National Association for Bilingual Education
(NABE)**
Union Center Plaza
810 1st St. NE, 3rd fl.
Washington, DC 20002

**National Association for
Chicano Studies (NACS)**
14 East Cuche LaPoundre
Colorado Springs, CO 80903
(509) 359-2404

**National Association for
Multicultural Education (NAME)**
c/o Donna M. Gollnick
National Council for Accreditation of
  Teacher Education
2010 Massachusetts Ave., NW, Suite 500
Washington, DC 20036
(202) 466-7496

National Council of La Raza
20 F. St. NW
Washington, DC 20001
(202) 289-1380

National Gay and Lesbian Task Force (NGLTF)
2320 17 St. NW
Washington, DC 20009
(202) 332-6483
http://www.ngltf.org/ngltf

National Organization for Women (NOW)
1000 16th St. NW, Suite 700
Washington, DC 20036
(202) 331-0066
http://www.now.org

National Rainbow Coalition
1700 K St. NW
Washington, DC 20005
(202) 728-1180
http://www.cais.com/rainbow

National Urban League (NUL)
500 E. 62nd St.
New York, NY 10021
(212) 310-9000
http://www.nul.org

National Women's History Project
7738 Bell Rd., Dept. E
Windsor, CA 95492
(707) 838-6000
http://www.nwhp.org/about.html

Native American Rights Fund
1506 Broadway
Boulder, CO 80302
(303) 447-8760
http://www.narf.org

Oxfam America
26 West St.
Boston, MA 02111
(617) 482-1211

Parents and Friends of Lesbians and Gays (PFLAG)
1012 14th St. NW, Suite 700
Washington, DC 20005
(202) 638-4200
http://www.pflag.org

People for the American Way
2000 M St. NW, Suite 400
Washington, DC 20036
(202) 467-4999
http://www.pfaw.org

Prejudice Institute/Center for the Applied Study of Ethnoviolence
712 West Lombard St.
Baltimore, MD 21201
(410) 706-5170

Puerto Rican Legal Defense and Education Fund
99 Hudson St.
New York, NY 10003
(212) 219-3360

Southeast Asia Resource Action Center (SEARAC)
1628 16th St. NW, 3rd Floor
Washington, DC 20009
(202) 667-4690
http://www.interaction.org/mb/searac.html

Southern Christian Leadership Conference (SCLC)
334 Auburn Ave, NE
Atlanta, GA 30312
(404) 522-1420

Southern Poverty Law Center
400 Washington St.
Montgomery, AL 36104
(334) 264-0286

Third Wave
185 Franklin St., 3rd Floor
New York, NY 10002
(212) 925-3400

Women's Legal Defense Fund
1875 Connecticut Ave. NW, Suite 710
Washington, DC 20009
(202) 986-2600

Women's Project
2224 S. Main
Little Rock, AK 72206
(501) 372-5113

Appendix D

Resources for Responsible Investing

1. Banking

For a list of minority-owned banks, contact

Federal Reserve Board
20th and C St., NW
Washington, DC 20002
(202) 452-3684

2. Community Development Credit Unions (CDCU)

CDCUs are financial cooperatives that serve and support low-income, often minority, members. For information about CDCUs in general and to locate one in your area, contact

National Federation of Community Development Credit Unions
120 Wall St., 10th Floor
New York, NY 10005
(212) 809-1850

3. Community Development Loan Funds (CDLF)

CDLFs are committed to grassroots efforts to build businesses and institutions in low-income communities. For information and a list of individual funds, contact

> National Association of Community Development Loan Funds
> 924 Cherry St., 3rd Floor
> Philadelphia, PA 19107
> (215) 923-4754

4. Money Markets and Mutual Funds

Among the numerous institutions that offer socially responsible money market and/or mutual funds are

> Calvert Group
> 4550 Montgomery Ave., Suite 1000 N
> Bethesda, MD 20814
> (800) 368-2748

> Citizens Trust
> 1 Harbour Place
> Suite 525
> Portsmouth, NH 03801
> (800) 533-3862 or (800) 223-7010

> Lincoln Investment Planning, Inc.
> Rightime Social Awareness Fund
> Forst Pavilion
> 218 Glenside Ave.
> Wyncote, PA 19095
> (800) 242-1421

> Parnassus Fund
> 1 Market — Stuart Tower, Suite 1600
> San Francisco, CA 94105
> (800) 999-3505

Vermont National Bank
Socially Responsible Banking Department
100 Main St.
P.O. Box 804
Brattleboro, VT 05302
(800) 772-3863

5. Affinity Credit Cards/Telephone Service

The Working Assets VISA card, which calls itself a "socially responsible credit card," contributes a percentage of its assets to a range of nonprofit organizations. For a credit card application, call the toll-free number for Working Assets: (800) 522-7759. For information on Working Assets Long Distance, which provides a donation for nonprofit groups each time you make a call, and at no extra cost to you, call: (800) 788-8588.

6. Socially Responsible Financial Planning/Consulting

First Affirmative Financial Network
1040 S. 8th St., Suite 200
Colorado Springs, CO 80906
(800) 422-7284

7. Books on Responsible Investing

Brill, Jack A., and Alan Reder. *Investing from the Heart: The Guide to Socially Responsible Investments and Money Management.* New York: Crown Publishers, 1992.

Harrington, John. *Investing with Your Conscience.* New York: John Wiley, 1992.

Meeker-Lowry, Susan. *Economics as If the Earth Really Mattered: A Catalyst Guide to Socially Conscious Investing.* Philadelphia: New Society Publishers, 1988.

Socially Responsible Financial Planning Handbook
available from:

Co-op America
1612 K St., NW, Suite 600
Washington, DC 20006
(202) 872-5307